WINDOWS 11

*Discover From Beginner to Expert with this
Ultimate& Complete Step-by-Step User Guide to
Learn &
Fully Enjoy Windows 11. Tips & Tricks to Master
Microsoft's New Operating System*

Table of Contents

INTRODUCTION TO WINDOWS 11 9

WHAT IS WINDOWS 11? 9
SOME RECOMMENDED LAPTOPS WITH WINDOWS 11 9
SYSTEM REQUIREMENTS FOR WINDOWS 11 11
FEATURES OF WINDOW 11 12
WHAT MAKES THE WINDOWS 11 ANY SPECIAL OR DIFFERENT? 15

HOW TO INSTALL AND DOWNLOAD 19

REQUIREMENTS FOR INSTALLING AND USING WINDOWS 11 19
HOW TO INSTALL WINDOWS 11 INSIDER PREVIEW 20
STEPS TO TAKE TO DOWNLOAD AND INSTALL WINDOWS 11 21
DOWNLOAD AND INSTALL THE PC HEALTH CHECK 23

HOW TO CUSTOMIZE THE START MENU IN WINDOWS 11 ...25

CUSTOMIZING THE START MENU 25
ADD FOLDERS IN THE START MENU 25
HOW TO ORGANIZE PINNED APPLICATIONS 25
PINNING APPS TO WINDOWS 26
HOW TO VIEW DRIVE USAGE IN WINDOWS 11 26
CHANGING THE LABEL OF YOUR DRIVE 26
REPOSITIONING ICONS 27
HOW TO USE THE RECYCLE BIN 28
HOW TO CUSTOMIZE THE DESKTOP 28
HOW TO ACCESS THE DISPLAY SETTINGS 30
PERSONALIZE YOUR DESKTOP ENVIRONMENT 30
WINDOWS 11 WIDGETS 31
HOW TO RESIZE WIDGETS 32
HOW TO UNINSTALL APPS FROM THE START MENU 33
HOW TO INSTALL THE WINDOWS UPDATE 33
HOW TO CUSTOMIZE LOOK AND FEEL 34
HOW TO DELETE AN APP 35

KNOW HOW TO STORE AND ORGANIZE FILES IN WINDOWS
11 37

HOW TO MOVE A FILE 37
HOW TO CREATE A COMPRESSED FILE 38
HOW TO SHOW THE RECENT FILES, APPS AND FOLDERS IN THE START 38
HOW TO REMOVE YOUR IMPORTANT DOCUMENTS AND APPS FROM
RECOMMENDED 38
HOW TO EXTRACT A ZIP FILE 39
THE CONTEXT MENU 39

How to Show Hidden Files and Folders in Windows 11......................39

UNDERSTANDING FOLDERS AND ICONS ON WINDOWS 11.41

How to Open Folder Option 41
Reinstall the Software 42
How to Open File Explorer Using Ribbons in Windows 11................42
How to Open the Folder Option in Windows 11...............................43
Removing Administrator Using Command Prompt............................44
Adding and Removing Quick Settings In Windows............................44
How to Change Administrator through the Control Panel 44
How to Change Administrator Using the Command Prompt............45
How to Remove a Setting from Quick Settings..............................45

HOW TO WORK WITH PROGRAMS, FILES AND APPS IN WINDOWS 11..47

How to Open and Manage Applications 47
How to Use the Taskbar Manager..48
How to Switch to Different Apps In Windows 11...............................48
How to Use Window Search 49
How to Customize Search Options..49
Windows Explorer and Management 50
How to Remove Unwanted Applications from Your Computer.........52
How to Adjust the Sound Settings and Sound Volume......................53
How to Use a Task Manager to Troubleshoot 54

HOW TO MANAGE DISK STORAGE ON WINDOWS 11............57

Search for Storage Details 57
How to Change Your PC Name in Windows 11 57
How to View Drive Usage 58
Changing the Label of Your Drive 59
Changing the label Using Disk Management....................................59
Changing the Label Using File Explorer..61

UNDERSTANDING PARTITION IN WINDOWS 11 62

How to Create a Partition on Windows 11 62
How to Extend a Partition on Windows 11 64
How to Increase/Decrease the Partition Size 67
How to Format or Delete the Partition 67
Using the Search and New Emojis..68
How to Use Transparency Effects..68
Disable Windows 11's Transparency Effects 70

HOW TO USE THE KEYBOARD IN WINDOWS 11....................71

How to Customize Touch Keyboard in Windows 11 71
How to Change Keyboard Settings 71
Using Handwriting and Various Keyboard Layouts 72

How to Use the Search 72
How to Use Clipboard Paste as Text 73
What are the Different Types of Files that Can Be Stored in
Clipboard? 73
Enabling the Clipboard History in Windows 11 73
How to Use Emojis in Touch Keyboard 74
How to Use Voice Typing in Touch Keyboard 75
What to Do If Search Stops Working 75
How to Use Several Keyboard Layouts 76
Changing the Keyboard Layout 77
Adding a Keyboard Layout 78
Removing a Keyboard Layout 78
How to Activate Input Indicator 79

UNDERSTANDING THE TASKBAR IN WINDOWS 11 80

How to Pin and Unpin Apps on the Taskbar 80
Quick Settings 82
How to Customize Your Quick Settings Flyout 83
How to Move Taskbar to the Top of the Screen 85
How to Perform a System Restore in Windows 11 87
How to Personalize the Taskbar in Windows 11 87
How to Tie an Application to the Taskbar in Windows 11 87
Multiple Desktop 88
How to Attach an Application to the Taskbar in Windows 11 88
Widgets Icon 89
New Family and Entertainment Widgets 90
Eliminate Pinned Programs and Items from the Taskbar in
Windows 11 90
Shift the Taskbar Items to the Left from the Center to the Left ... 91
How Do I Hide or Show Taskbar corner symbols in Windows 11? 91
Overflow and Taskbar Corner Icons 91
Ungrouping Icons in the Taskbar in Windows 11 91
Add an App to Taskbar 93
How to Boot Your PC in Safe Mode 93
How to Change Administrator on Windows 1 Using the Control
Panel 93
How to Fix Desktop Crashes in Windows 11 93
How to Go Back to Windows 10 94
How to Use Cleanup Recommendations 95
Archive apps 95

DIFFERENCES BETWEEN WINDOWS 10 AND WINDOWS 11 . 97

New UI and Design 97
Widgets 98
New Features in Calculator App 98
Calendar and Mail 99

FILE EXPLORER..99
MULTITASKING HAS BEEN ENHANCED 99
ENHANCED TOUCHSCREEN INPUT 100
NEW MICROSOFT EDGE FEATURES..100
AUGMENTED COLLABORATION 101
INTEGRATION WITH ANDROID APPS...102
MICROSOFT STORE 102
ENHANCEMENTS TO GAMEPLAY...102
IN WINDOWS 11, MICROSOFT TEAMS VS. SKYPE FOR BUSINESS..................103
OTHER NOTABLE DISTINCTIONS 104

FILE EXPLORER IN WINDOWS 11 105

HOW TO FIX CRASHING FILE EXPLORER.....................................105
HOW TO USE SNAP LAYOUT IN DIFFERENT APPS 106
HOW TO HIDE THE WINDOWS 11 TASKBAR 107
HOW TO ENTER BIOS IN WINDOWS 11 107
FINDING YOUR IP ADDRESS IN WINDOWS 11 107

THE WINDOWS 11 SUBSYSTEM FOR LINUX......................109

HOW TO INSTALL WINDOWS SUBSYSTEM FOR LINUX (WSL) ON WINDOWS11
.... 109

VIRTUAL MACHINE IN WINDOWS 11.....................................111

HOW TO USE THE VIRTUAL DESKTOP.......................................111
ACTIVATE VIRTUALIZATION IN BIOS 112
INSTALL WINDOWS 11 ON YOUR COMPUTER 113
INSTALLING AND SETTING UP WINDOWS 11 ON RASPBERRY PI 4 113
HOW TO ENABLE BLUETOOTH THROUGH SETTINGS 114
HOW TO USE THE WINDOWS TROUBLESHOOTER TO REPAIR BLUETOOTH ... 114
HOW TO SCREENSHOT ON WINDOWS 11 114

NETWORKING IN WINDOWS 11..116

IP ADDRESSES AND CONFIGURATION 118
DYNAMIC AND STATIC IP ADDRESSES......................................119
HOW TO CONNECT TO A WI-FI NETWORK IN WINDOWS 11 120
HOW TO CONNECT TO THE INTERNET 123
SETTING UP A VPN..126

ANDROID APPLICATIONS IN WINDOWS 11........................128

HOW TO INSTALL ANDROID APPLICATIONS ON WINDOWS 11 128
ANDROID WINDOWS SUBSYSTEM 130

(CPU) CENTRAL PROCESSING UNIT IN WINDOWS 11 133

HOW TO BOOST YOUR PROCESSOR OR CPU SPEED ON WINDOWS 11..........133
HOW TO FACTORY RESET ON WINDOWS 11..................................136

WINDOWS 11 SECURITY SETTING...140

How to Customize Privacy Setting 140
How to Use Quick Setting Center... 142
How to Change a Default Printer 144
How to Connect to Windows 11 Store 144
How to Change Your Windows Password 146
How to Lock Your Computer.. 146
Window Security Settings 147
Using a Password Manager 150
How to Disable OneDrive.. 151
Set Up a Second Email Address for Your Microsoft Account 151
Decide What Services You Share with Microsoft............................. 151
How to Set a Microsoft Account Password 152
Windows Defender Security Center.. 152
How to Add Windows Defender to Your Desktop............................ 155
What Is Windows Defender Antivirus? 156
Antivirus Protection... 157
Other Options 159
How to Connect and Extend to an External Display 159
How to Connect to a Windows PC and Mirror the Screen from an
Android Device.. 161
How to Cast or Connect to An External Device 162
How to Connect to a Windows PC and Mirror the Screen from an
Android Device.. 163

WORKING WITH FONTS IN WINDOWS 11 166

Downloading and Installing Fonts Manually in Windows 11 166
Activate the Font File 167
Display Options 168
Monitor Menu.. 169
Helpful Inclusion in Windows 11.. 169
How to install Fonts via Settings in Windows 11 or 10 169

WINDOWS 11 SHORTCUTS KEYS, TIPS AND TRICKS 170

Tips and Tricks 171
Basic Troubleshooting.. 171
Servicing and Deployment 174
How to Clone HDD to SSD in Windows 11 175
Using Task Manager and Ctrl-Alt-Del... 175
System Configuration Utility (MSconfig)....................................... 177

CONCLUSION 179

ALPHABETICAL INDEX 181

Introduction To Windows 11

What Is Windows 11?

Windows 11 is the new version of the Windows operating system developed by Microsoft. It was announced on the **24**th of June and was launched on the **5**th of October. It is the most significant update to the Windows operating system since the release of Windows 10 in 2015. It was launched as a free upgrade to users running on Windows 10. Windows 11 was designed to promote and inspire creat ivity and productivity.

It includes some compelling new features such as being able to download and run Android applications, attractive designs, good and better security, better PC gaming experiences, ease of use, and creativity. Unlike the other Windows where you locate your systemsoftware locally on your computer, Windows 11 gives you access to keep all the key components in the cloud storage.

However, over the coming months, Microsoft will be notifying every user when the update is available for them. To Microsoft's credit, the Windows team has done an excellent job IN bringing this particular operating system of which the flaws of the previous Windows operating system are no longer an issue.

Some Recommended Laptops with Windows 11

Acer Nitro 5

Asus ProArt Studiobook One

Dell Inspiron 14

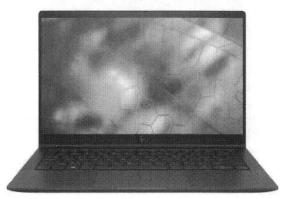

HP Elite Dragonfly

Lenovo Legion

System Requirements for Windows 11

The minimum system requirements for Windows 11, as published by Microsoft, are listed thus:

- Processor: 1GHz or faster. 2 or more cores on a compatible 64-bit processor or system on a chip (SoC).
- RAM: 4 GB minimum.
- Storage: 64 GB minimum.
- Display: 9" or greater display screen, high definition display (720p).
- Graphics card: DirectX 12 or higher, with a WDDM 2.0 driver.
- Security: UEFI firmware, secure boot and TPM version 2.0 compatible.

Microsoft is officially retiring 32-bit Windows, with the launch of the Windows 11 OS. 32-bit Windows apps will continue to enjoy support. However, older PCs are not expected to meet Windows 11 stringent requirements for processors. Two or higher cores on a 64-bit processor will be good to go. PCs built since 2019 will pass all the Windows 11 compatibility requirements. However, there are some exceptions from older generation PCs.

Most PCs built from around 2015 have hardware security components called the Trusted Platform Module (TPM 2.0) support. There might be a need to enable this in the firmware setting if this is not already done.

Devices with display screens smaller than 9 inches will not work with the new Operating System.

For Windows 10, a minimum storage of 16 GB and a minimum 2 GB RAM were required. With Windows 11, however, minima of 64 GB and 4 GB are required respectively for the storage and the RAM. This means that a PC with lesser configuration will need to be fixed, before upgrading to the latest version.

A steady Internet connection is required to keep Windows 11 up to date, as there are features that will not work without it.

PCs and devices, which do not meet up with the minimum requirements of Windows 11, can install the Windows 11 Insider Preview on their devices to receive updates pending when Windows 11 is officially released. In section 1.2 of this Guide, how to install Windows 11 Insider Preview is discussed.

Features of Window 11

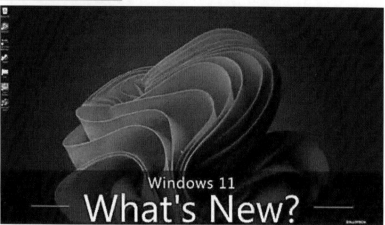

Windows 11 introduced new features compared to its predecessors. Some of these features include the ability to download and run Android apps on your Windows PC, as well as upgrades to Microsoft Teams, the Start menu, and the software's overall style, which is cleaner and more Mac-like. However, not all of the functions are available right now. Here are the features of Windows 11:

- *Android Apps:* While other versions of Windows have never supported Android apps. Microsoft has announced that Windows 11 will support Android applications and are installable from within the new Microsoft store via Amazon Appstore. This means that there will be a better and great performance, easy downloading and updating of apps.

- *Microsoft Teams:* Users can now use Chat from Microsoft Teams. You can start a video call or chat with your friends and family. With this feature, you will be able to sign in, add contacts and connect either via individual or group chats. The chat icon is located on the taskbar. You can click on it when you want to connect with someone. You will also see your recent chats with your friends and be able to start a new call or chat.

- *Snap Group:* A new feature that allows you to group programs and windows for easier organization. It is similar to how you group apps on Android and iOS, or how you can use split-screen on Windows.

- *Focus Assists Updates*: Windows 11 has added Focus assist as a part of the Clock app. This is a feature that removes distraction, enables you to control notifications, and avoids disturbance from apps. It stops notifications from popping up on your screen. It is activated automatically when you are duplicating your display, playing a game, or using an app in full-screen mode.

- *Multiple desktop/workspaces:* This feature is already available on Windows 10 but it is now much easier to use in Windows 11. To create multiple desktops, click on the *Task View* on the taskbar and select *New Desktop*. Desktops provide more space for your programs without the need for additional physical monitors. You can make separate desktops for business, school, and private use. You can as well customize their background.

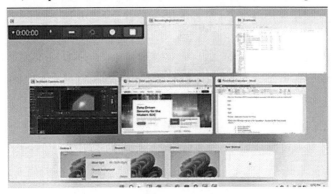

- *New Windows keyboard shortcuts*: Windows introduced new keyboard shortcuts that will help its users work faster and more efficiently. You can use Windows 10 shortcuts on Windows 11 but the latest OS version includes various new keyboard shortcuts that provide quick access to new features like Quick settings, Snap layouts, Widgets, and Notification Center. Below are some of the new keyboard shortcuts

- *Windows key + N:* This opens the Notification Center layout. All your notifications and a full-month calendar view are all in the Notification Center.

- *Windows key + Z:* This opens the Snap layout menu. The Snap layout menu is a new feature that helps users to organize apps and windows by grouping them. It brings up a menu with different grids when hovering over the maximize button. You can have up to six layouts and that depends on the size of your screen

- *Windows key + A:* This opens the Quick Setting fly out. This is where you manage common PC settings quickly and easily like Volume, Bluetooth, Wi-Fi, Brightness. You can also find media playback controls that appear when you play music with Microsoft Edge.

- *Windows key + W:* This opens the Widgets interface

- *WIDGETS:* Widgets is a new feature in Windows 11 that consists of different types of information like news, sports results, weather, traffic, stocks.

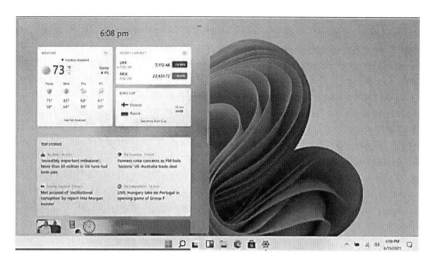

What Makes the Windows 11 Any Special or Different?

Remember how it feels like hearing an old story being retold over and over again ? I guess we can all tell the end from the very beginning. I mean, it takes away all the fun elements because we have heard it too many times. Boring right?

With the rise in technological improvements, a lot of us might have given up on the quest to keep up. I guess we are all getting used to being "mind blown" to the point that we no longer are in fact, mind blown. We have probably seen it all. Or maybe not.

When Windows 10 was launched, I thought that had to be the peak of it all, but recently, with Microsoft announcing its newest release; The Windows 11, the new features it is endowed with would fascinate even the most uninterested.

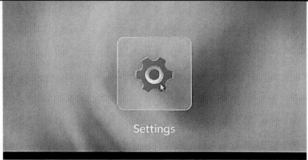

There's also the new action center and a new notification Centre which looks good.

Want to hear something interesting? These are not even the most intriguing elements of Windows 11. The upgrade brings with it some delightful features which we will be talking about shortly.

First of all, let's discuss the new Microsoft store. The first thing that catches your eye is the way the new layout and UI harmonize with the whole new modern Windows 11 design. Take a look at this:

If we put this side by side with the UI of the former store, we can tell that the former looked a bit clustered up in comparison. And this looks way better if we would admit. It is also said to be faster and more responsive and the search mechanism is way better too. But hey! Check this out;

The new Microsoft store will allow all types of apps, ranging from the modern universal apps, web apps, and very importantly, Windows 32 traditional apps like Adobe or a browser like Chrome. This makes sense because developers can choose to use Microsoft payment systems or their own and they don't have to give any cuts to Microsoft.

Now this one is for the movie freaks. Just kidding. For everyone who loves a good relaxation. The Microsoft store's entertainment tab will now list movies and shows from different platforms, making it a great one-stop place!

It just gets even more exciting. Windows 11 will now be supportin g Android apps. First of all, Android apps will be available from the Microsoft store which is amazing.

This is proof. The picture above shows TikTok working on Windows 11.

One other thing about Windows 11 is that the desktop version is way better. Now, you can personalize them with different apps and different wallpapers to give all of them a very unique look.

I video call or a virtual meeting is now easier to do on Windows with the developed feature called Microsoft Teams. Users can now make calls on the go just by clicking on the Teams icon and selecting a contact. Yes, it is that easy.

It is a good season for gamers too. With the gaming features integrated, Windows 11 is also a big update for gamers. Starting from the new feature called auto HDR which automatically updates games with better lighting and more vibrant colors, to the direct storage which is basically games loading assets on the GPU, which means games launching speed and loading times are a lot faster.

How to Install and Download Windows 11

Before you consider downloading and installing the new Windows 11, you need to check if your system meets the requirements needed. The best way to do this is to download the PC health check. This app will give you a rundown of all the requirements and also show you if your system meets the requirement and what you can do to ensure it meets the requirement if it doesn't.

After being certified eligible by PC health check simply type settings in your search bar and then click on windows updates and finally click on update windows. If your system meets the requirement you will click on download and install.

It's worth noting that you must have a stable internet connection before you can download this update on your system.

Requirements for Installing and Using Windows 11

Everyone seems excited about the recent update by Microsoft with the release of Windows 11 but the question is will you be able to enjoy this new update too? Will your laptop be able to run it or will you need to purchase another one?

Here is a list of requirements your system needs to meet to enable it to run the new Windows 11

Specifications	Requirements
Processor	1GHZ or faster with at least 2 cores running on a compatible 64-bit processor or system on a chip
RAM	At least 4GB
Storage	You should have at least 64GB of storage on your device
System Firmware	UEFI, Secure Boot capable
Trusted Platform Module(TPM)	At least version 2.0
Graphics Card	Should be compatible with DirectX 12 or a later version with WDDM 2.0 driver

19

Display	Your system should possess HD(720p) with a display greater than 9 inches diagonally and at least 8bits per color channel

You can also use the Microsoft PC Health Check app to find out if your computer is eligible. This way you know if you are good to go or need to buy another PC to use the new Windows. The Microsoft PC Health will also help you find out if you have or need to enable the Trusted Mobile Module version 2.0 which is a compulsory eligibility requirement and can be the only stumbling block as regards the eligibility of your laptop.

How to Install Windows 11 Insider Preview

Windows 11 is speculated to be released in October 2021. Some individuals already have access to the OS, even though it is yet to be released. These are you and I. In other words, anyone can have this privilege if you follow the steps below. The only way possible to get access to the new Windows 11 beta is to be part of the Windows Insider Program and have an active Microsoft account.

The following will show you how to be a member of the Windows 11 Insider Program, after which this guide will show you how to install the Windows 11 beta.

Step 1: Open *Settings* on your PC with Windows 10 OS.

Step 2: Go to Update & Security *and click on* Windows Insider Program *from the left.*

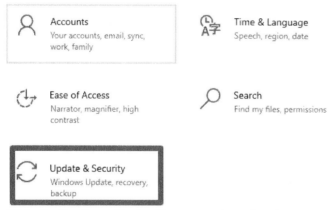

Step 3: Click the *Get Started* button if you are not yet signed up.

Step 4: Click *Link an Account* when the pop-up comes up

Step 5: Log-in with your details or click on an already registered account

Step 6: On the screen that appears next, you are to pick between *Dev Channel* or *Beta Channel*.

Step 7: If bugs are a concern and your PC's stability too, then it is recommended you pick Beta Channel.

Step 8: Press *Confirm* on the screen that appears next.

Step 9: Restart your PC to complete your sign-up, either *now* or *later.*

Steps to Take to Download and Install Windows 11

When the installation process has been completed and your PC restarted, then you are now a member of the Windows Insider Program. You can go ahead to install the Windows 11 beta, by following the steps below:

Step 1: Go to *Settings.*

Step 2: Then to Update & Security.

Step 3: Click on Check for Updates *on the* Windows Update *tab.*

21

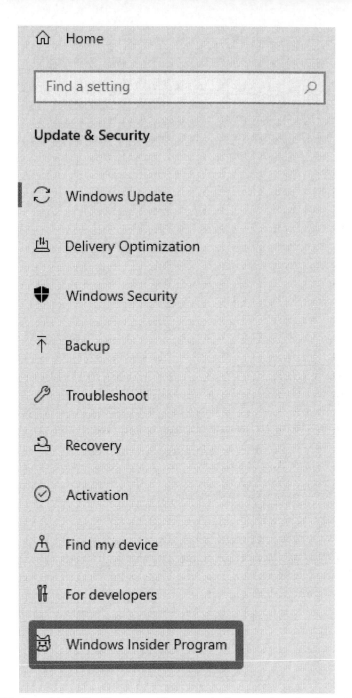

⌂ Home

Find a setting 🔍

Update & Security

🔄 Windows Update

🔔 Delivery Optimization

🛡 Windows Security

↑ Backup

🔧 Troubleshoot

🗄 Recovery

✓ Activation

👤 Find my device

🏗 For developers

🖥 Windows Insider Program

Step 4: Windows 11 Insider Preview will automatically start downloading after a few seconds.

Step 5: You will be prompted to restart your PC when the download is complete.

Step 6: After the PC has installed the update, the Windows 11 beta will be ready to use right away; and all the files and apps on the PC will remain intact.

Download and Install the PC Health Check

Once installed and launched, the home page which says PC at a glance appears

At the top of the page, identify the section that says *Introducing Windows 11* and click the blue box which reads *Check now.*

At this point, you will be notified by a small dialog box if perhaps your pc does not meet the requirement. The message in the dialog box will conventionally say: *This PC can't run Windows.*

However, if your machine is compatible, you can download the update for free.

As an alternative to the PC Health app, you can manually check the list of requirements placed on the Microsoft website.

Minimum system requirements

Processor	1 gigahertz (GHz) or faster with 2 or more cores on a compatible 64-bit processor or System on a Chip (SoC)	Graphics card	DirectX 12 compatible graphics / WDDM 2.x
Memory	4 GB RAM	Display	>9" with HD Resolution (720p)
Storage	64 GB or larger storage device	Internet connection	Microsoft account and internet connectivity required for setup for Windows 11 Home
System firmware	UEFI, Secure Boot capable		
TPM	Trusted Platform Module (TPM) version 2.0		Certain features require specific hardware, see detailed system requirements.

Shop for a Windows 11 compatible PC at these retailers[4] [5]

Best Buy	Amazon	Walmart	Microsoft Store
BUY ONLINE >	BUY ONLINE >	BUY ONLINE >	BUY ONLINE >

23

The problem with this method is that it might be a little hard as one may not know where to check for each of these values and so, the WhyNotWin11 app proves to be a better alternative.

The WhyNotWin11 is a free and open-source tool that will tell us whether a computer qualifies. And you can download it at the website-whynotwin11.org.

The website will take us to the Github repository for the tool as seen below;

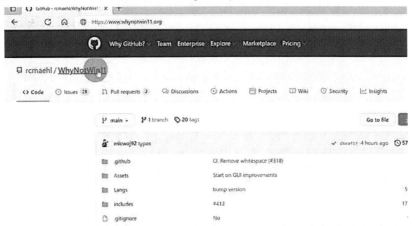

To download the tool, simply scroll down a little bit more till you see *Download latest stable release.* Click on that button and once you finish downloading, navigate to your download folder and double click on the *WhynotWin11.exe.* This immediately launches the compatibility results.

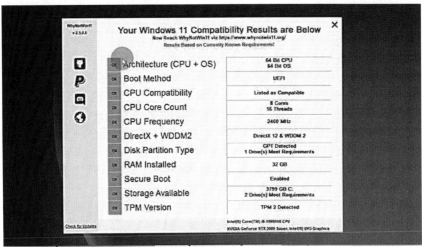

This shows how the system compares against the system requirements that Microsoft has published. The indication of color green shows positive compatibility.

These are the ways to check if one's system is compatible with the Windows 11 update.

How to Customize the Start Menu in Windows 11

Customizing the Start Menu

To access the Start Menu on Windows 11, you can either click on the *Start Menu* icon on the taskbar or press the *Windows key*. The Start Menu will display your often-used apps, recently-added apps, Jump Lists, File Explorer and recently-opened items in Start.

In order to change the Start Menu on Windows 11 to suit your taste, follow the steps below: *Step 1:* Press *Windows key + I* to go to *Settings*.

Step 2: Then find *Personalization*.

Step 3: Open the *Start* page.

Step 4: Then change the Start Menu to the way you want it.

You can add folders you want to appear in the Start Menu here.

Add Folders in the Start Menu

Follow the below to start adding folders in the Start Menu

Step 1: **Press down** *Windows key* + *I* **or go to** *Settings* from the *Start Menu*.

Step 2: Then find *Personalization*.

Step 3: Open the *Start* page.

Step 4: Go to *Folders*.

That is, *Settings* > *Personalization* > *Start* > *Folders* On the *Folders settings*, customize by turning on and off the options, as you desired.

How to Organize Pinned Applications

Your pinned apps will spill to multiple pages, and you might want to re-arrange them to your order of preference. To do this, follow the steps below:

Step 1: Click the *Start* button on the taskbar or press the *Windows key* to bring out the *Start menu*.

Step 2: Then browse through your pinned apps to select the particular one you want moved.

Step 3: Right-click on the app, and select *Move to Top*

Pinning Apps to Windows

1. Go to the bottom of the screen
2. Click on *search*
3. Click on the *name of an app*
4. Right click on the *app*
5. *Select pin* to taskbar

How to View Drive Usage in Windows 11

When Windows Settings opens, select the *System category* from the left sidebar...

After that, Windows 11 will display total/used storage by file types.

While you are on the Storage settings, you can turn *on* the toggle switch beside the "Storage Sense" option.

Changing the Label of Your Drive

Follow the steps below to change the name or label of your drive:

Open *Settings* from the Start Menu.

Then, click on *System*.

Then click on *Storage* on your left-hand pane.

Afterwards, click on *Advanced storage settings* from your right-hand pane.

Find *Disk & volumes* on your right-hand side and click on it.

Locate the specific drive you want renamed and click on its icon.

All the partitions of the drive will appear. Highlight the partition with the biggest size.
Then click on *Properties*.

Data Volume section will then come up.

Click on the *Change label*.

Type the new letter in the space provided.

And finally click *Ok* to conclude the renaming.

It is important to use a different letter from the ones already used.

Press down *Windows key+ E* keys to go to the File section to see what letters or labels
are already in use. Then click on *This PC*, where all the drives connected to the PC
are.

Repositioning Icons

Change the icons by simply *right-clicking* on the *taskbar*.

This will take you to the taskbar's settings under which you will see a section called
the "*Taskbar behaviors*"

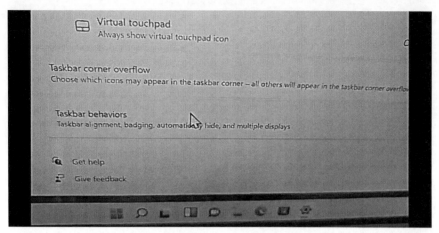

you will then *select* "*Taskbar alignment*" to move the icons to either the left or the center.

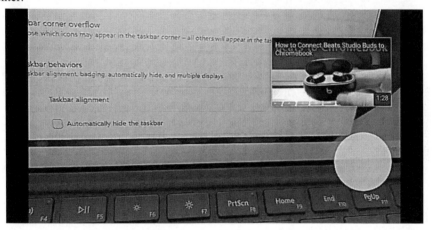

How to Use the Recycle Bin

One of the key components of the desktop is access to the recycle bin. So typically, anytime you delete something from your computer, it will automatically put it in a recycled bin. So if you want to retrieve something from a recycle bin, you can double click the recycle bin, and it will display what you have recently deleted. Then right - click on it and choose to restore it.

How to Customize the Desktop

To customize the desktop, right-click on the desktop and choose to personalize.

Then under personalize, you can change many different settings such as color, themes, lock screen, taskbar items, fonts, _etc_. That is where you personalize the background. You can pick different background photos, change contrasts, and do other functions. Think of it like you are modifying the settings on your smartphone to change the visual look and feel of the applications in there.

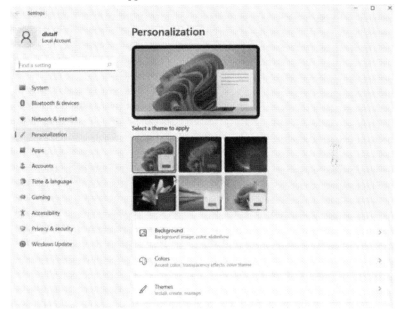

How to Access the Display Settings

The display setting is another functionality that you can access through the desktop by right-clicking anywhere on the screen. Suppose you wanted to change the font size on the monitor, the resolution, and so on. That is where you'll make those changes by right-clicking and choosing display settings.

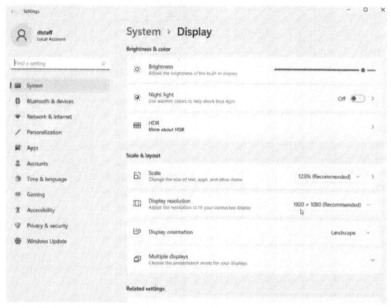

If you right-click again on the desktop, you will notice some additional options, and it is more like a look and feel of what used to be on Windows 10.

Personalize Your Desktop Environment

Snap Groups, Snap Layouts: Move your cursor over the maximize/minimize option when you start an application. You may then choose a new design for the application: You can change the size of programs on your desktop with this functionality. The snapped design also remains intact when you integrate other applications into the design.

When you save a Snap Layout with your applications, it becomes a Snap Group. When you mouse through an application in an established snap layout on the taskbar, it displays all of the applications in that particular layout. Snap Group is the name of this functionality. You may choose a group, and all of the applications will launch in the same way. You may switch across Snap Groups as you introduce more by choosing the Snap Group.

The *Settings app > System > Multitasking* may be used to control several snap capabilities.

Snap Layouts may also be added to applications that your company builds.

Start menu: By default, certain programs are set to the Start menu. You may chang e the appearance of the Start menu by setting (and unsetting) the applications you wish. You may, for instance, pin frequently used applications in your company, like Outlook, Microsoft Teams, Outlook, applications your company builds, and more.

You may use policy to distribute your personalized Start menu design to your company's computers.

The *Settings app > Personalization* allows users to customize several aspects of the Start menu.

Taskbar: The Taskbar allows you to unpin (and pin) applications. You may , for instance, pin frequently used applications in your company, like Microsoft Teams, Outlook, applications your company builds, and lots more.

You may deliver your personalized Taskbar to computers in your business using policies. The *Settings app > Personalization* allows you to customize several Taskbar functions.

Widgets: Widgets may be found on the Taskbar. It has a customizable feed with calendar, weather, news, stock prices, and other information: The Computer Configuration\Administrative Templates\Windows Components\widgets Group Policy may be used to disable or enable this capability. You may also create a personalized Taskbar for your company's computers.

Virtual Desktops: To develop a new desktop, click the Desktops symbol on the Taskbar: Based on what you are doing, utilize the desktop to launch different programs. You may, for instance, build a Travel workstation that comprises travel-related applications and websites.

You can launch a personalized Taskbar to computers in your company using policies.

The Settings app > System > Multitasking allows you to control several desktop functionalities.

Windows 11 Widgets

Widgets are essentially a group of small graphical apps, quickly accessible directly from the Windows 11 taskbar and designed to provide at-a-glance information about news, weather, sports results, stocks, *etc.* The widget's menu can be customized to only show the widgets you want, and include a Bing search bar that will open results in a new browser window.

What widget does in Windows 11?

While there are no third-party widgets, there is a handful that you can pick and choose to display on your menu. Here are all the widgets currently available in the Windows 11 Insider Preview build:

Calendar: It shows you the current date and lists any upcoming events you've added.

Entertainment: lists films and TV shows that have recently been released on the Microsoft Store.

Photos: cycles through photos and images saved to your Microsoft account.

Sports: displays current sports scores and recent results. You can adjust which leagues and teams are shown.

Tips: provides brief advice for using various Microsoft software, including Windows11 and Edge.

To Do: This allows you to create a list of tasks and displays it in the widgets menu. You can mark individual tasks as completed.

Traffic: displays a small map and describes the traffic conditions in your area.

Watchlist: shows stock values. Similar to the Sports widget, you can choose which stocks should appear.

Weather: shows current weather conditions in your area, as well as the forecast for the following three days.

There is also a larger "Top Stories" box towards the bottom of the widgets menu, which pulls headlines from a range of news sources

How to Resize Widgets

When it comes to resizing, Windows 11 offers you three size options, Small, Medium, or Large. However, changing the size only affects the length of the widget title and not its width. This can be construed as a drawback by many.

To resize the widget, first, click on the ellipsis at its top-right corner.

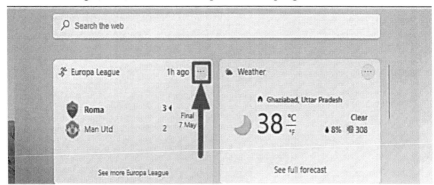

The first three options on the menu are to customize the size of the widget, select the desired option. The current size will have a dot before.

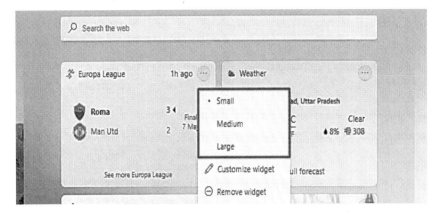

How to Uninstall Apps from the Start Menu

With Windows 11, you don't have to go to the control panel to uninstall an app as you can now do it from the start menu. To do this;

- Click on the Windows icon to display apps.
- To view more apps, click **all apps** at the top right corner.
- Right-click on an app you want to uninstall and tap uninstall.
- Confirm the action to uninstall the app.
- Remember that you cannot delete default apps.

How to Install the Windows Update

in this section, we will install the Windows updates and keep the computer up to date. Go under the Windows search or press the Windows key, then type Windows update. Notice that there are some updates. Click install, and the updates will be installed on the computer.

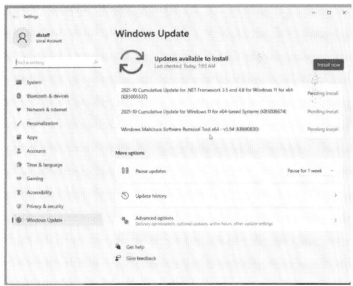

The other thing to remember is that you can pause Windows updates if you don't want the computer to be restarted during business hours or want to pause them for a week, and so on. That is where you can change those settings. If you want to look at the history of updates, you can click on Windows updates history, and it will show you what has been installed on the computer. Further down under advanced options, youcan also install the updates at certain hours of the day or at certain times. You can choose when to receive the Windows updates

Another option that you might want to consider under optional updates is drive r software for your pc or non-crucial updates for your pc. That might be helpful, but itis important to keep your pc up to date whether whatever version of Windows you have for security reasons, better performance of your pc, and sometimes additional functionality.

How to Customize Look and Feel

In this segment of Windows 11, we'll demonstrate how to customize the look and feel of Windows 11. There are a couple of ways you can do the changing of the look and feel. You can right-click on the desktop and then choose to personalize. Then under personalize, you can change and pick various themes. So let's say you want to utilize any of the themes. It will adjust all the colors and everything related to that Windows theme. If you want to further just customize certain things, such as in the desktop settings, change the sounds, change the defaults or the cursor, and so on. That is where you do it as well.

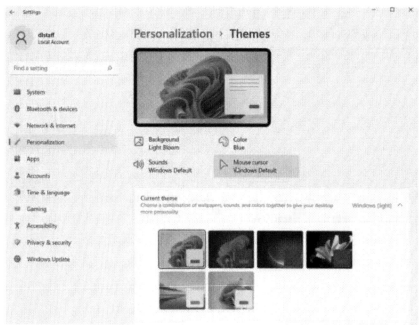

Now to change the font size of your icons and components of Windows, right -click on the desktop and choose display settings. Now we are going to demonstrate this from the desktop functionality. However, you can also search for it and choose display

settings. Then under the scaling, you can change it to be larger fonts and larger icons or smaller if you prefer and screen orientation and things of that nature.

How to Delete an App

If you need to delete an application for some reason, notice that it has changed in Windows 11. You can click on the three dots on the far right or in the configuration icon in the far right, then uninstall the app from the app & features.

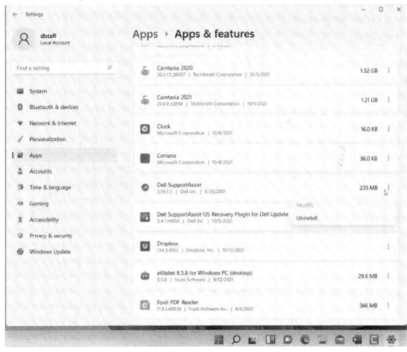

Additionally, you have the gaming settings, privacy settings, and Windows update. So all of that is very similar to an iPhone or a Smartphone, where you can change and customize the settings about your device. The same idea is here on windows 11 as well. You can also search on the search bar for a particular setting you are looking for. Let's say you're not sure where disk cleanup is located. You can still search for it. So that's how you access the Windows settings and customize settings related to Windows 11.

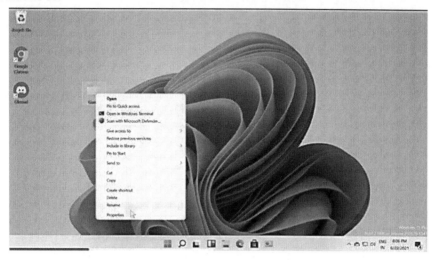

Know How to Store and Organize Files in Windows 11

Now when working with folders, most users don't fully understand working with files. Let's say you want to create a new folder, and if you click on new, you can choose to create a new shortcut, a new folder, or a new bunch of other things if you create just a new folder. So click on new and then choose folder. Then you have to name the folder, and then you hit enter.

How to Move a File

To move a file into a folder, you can do it a couple of ways. Let's say you have a file and you want to move it. You can drag it and then put it in that folder. That is called Drag and drop. It's great as long as you're precise in it. There's a danger in a drag and drop because sometimes, you may drop the file in the wrong place.

So the best way to move files around is by simply selecting them, and if they are more than one, you can either select all or select just a few of them or hold the control key and select random ones.

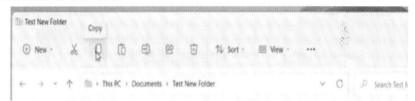

You can also right-click and then choose the cut options.

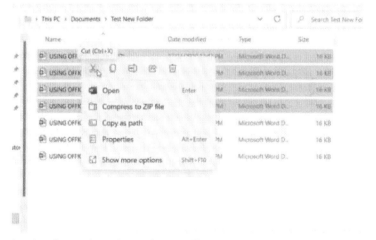

Then notice that the options changed as well in Windows 11. The icons don't show cut anymore or copy unless you hold the mouse on it. Then to move the file, click on cut and go back to the folder where you wish to paste the file. Then right-click and select the paste option. Notice again that the word paste is missing, but you have the icon to paste or the paste icon on the top. These may be very basic concepts, but it's really necessary to work effectively in the workplace.

How to Create a Compressed File

Now one of the needs that most users are not very familiar with in any version of Windows is how to create a compressed file or a zip file as it's called. So let's say you have Word 2019 folder, and it has a bunch of things inside. Assuming you want to send it to somebody in the compressed format because it has a lot of things in it.

To create a zip folder or a zip file, you have to right-click on the folder and click on Compress to zip file. Now the terminology in Windows 11 has changed, so you click on Create a zip file. It's going to do its thing and put all the files, including the folder and potentially subfolders, into one single file for you to send away.

Notice it has a zip folder with a little icon thing, and that's what you'd need to send. Still, you are sending one compressed package for large zip files. It's better than emailing them to share either using one drive or google drive or some iCloud file sharing platform. Most systems are not going to deliver emails that contain zip files for security reasons.

How to Show the Recent Files, Apps and Folders in the Start

The new Windows 11 gives you a few options to help you locate your files faster from the start menu.

To show recent files, folders and apps in the start;

- Right-click on your Windows display and click *Personalization.*

- On the next page, click *start.*

- To display recently added apps on the start menu, click on the *show recently added apps* toggle to turn the feature on.

- Click on *show most used apps* to turn it on or off.

- *To show recently opened apps, Click on* Show recently opened items instart, jump lists and file explorer.

- You can also choose what folders appear on start. Tap *folders* and selectcheck or uncheck different folders from the list.

How to Remove Your Important Documents and Apps from Recommended

For more privacy, you can prevent third party users from getting access to your important files in one click.

- Click on the Windows icon to open the start menu.
- Under recommended, click *more* for a list of your documents.
- Right-click on a file you wish to remove and select *Remove from list.*

How to Extract a Zip File

Now let's say that you received a file type with a zip file. You also need to extract those files. Notice there is an option for extracting all items in your folder, or you can right-click on it and choose to extract all. That's a necessary process for any zip files to open on your PC. It would be best if you do this only when you're completely sure from a safe sender.

Notice it's going to, by default, extract it in the same folder that you had it. However, you can change it to a different folder, click extract, and display all those files. Notice that it creates a new folder matching the zip folder. Then under that, there are actual files.

The Context Menu

The context menu for the file explorer and Windows 11 have changed. Notice the rounded corners, the visual look, and the feel. Then the options have been rearranged, and the icons have changed.

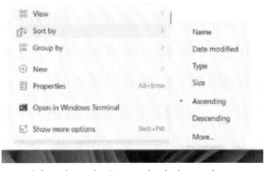

Most commonly used functions don't contain their words anymore. There are more options, which would bring more of the old look and feel from Windows 10, and that's where it used to look.

How to Show Hidden Files and Folders in Windows 11

Hidden files can help protect your privacy if you use your PC in a public environment; however, you can also choose not to hide files as well. To show hidden files on your Windows 11;

- Go to file explorer or simply click on **Windows key + E key** to do this.
- Click on the options icon at the top right side of the page. When the options under this icon opens, select **options.**
- Proceed to the **view** section under the **folder options.**
- **Check the button labelled** show hidden files, folders and drives.
- Click **Apply** and confirm selection by tapping **OK.**

However, there are files and folders there that are hidden by default. To view those files and folders, go to view, scroll down to show, and choose show hidden files.

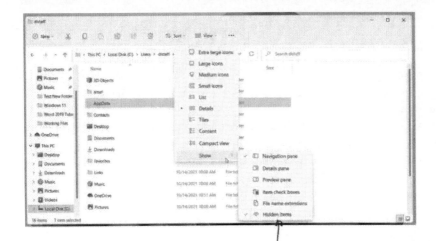

Understanding Folders and Icons on Windows 11

How to Open Folder Option

The new Windows, like every other edition of Windows since Windows 8, has the Windows Folder Options. This dialog box allows the user to configure all manner of settings, and change the preference for the File Explorer on the PC. To open Folder options, follow the steps below:

Step 1: Open File Explorer *Step 2:* You will see 3 at the top of the opened windows, click on *See More.*

Step 3: A drop-down menu will appear, click to open the options.

Step4: Here, a window with 3 tabs, like in previous editions, will appear: *General, View,* and *Search*.

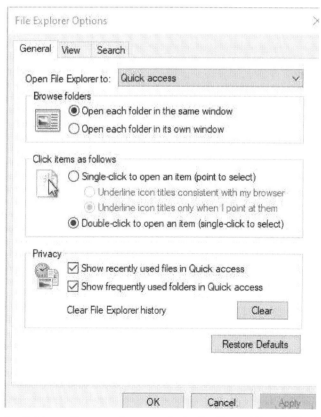

Alternatively, Folder options can be opened via the Control Panel. To do this, follow these steps: *Step 1:* open *Start.*

Step 2: Locate the *Control Panel* and click on it.

Step 3: *Then click on* Experience &

Personalization.

Step 4: Here just click *File Explorer* options and start customizing your experience.

Reinstall the Software

In case the solution discussed above fails to solve your problem, you can consid er reinstalling the software for a start. To do this, follow the prompts below:

- Right-click on the Start icon and then navigate to *Settings,* click on *Apps,* and then select *Apps & features*.

- Locate the specific program that keeps crashing, and tap the three (3) dots menu beside it.

- Click *Uninstall*.

- Tap the *Uninstall* button from another interface that will be displayed.

- Select *Yes* and proceed with the on-screen instruction to uninstall the software from your PC.

After you have uninstalled the software successfully, you can then proceed to download the setup file and install the software again. Then check whether the problem persists or not.

How to Open File Explorer Using Ribbons in Windows 11

Windows has an updated version of file explorer that retains same classic look but new menu that shows basic classic commands and making it more difficult to find them. A ribbon is a command bar that helps a program's features into a series of tabs at the top of a window. It has the capacity to replace both the traditional menu bar and toolbars. Ribbon tabs are made of groups, which are a labeled set of closely related commands.

To open file explorer with Ribbons, one has to do the following.

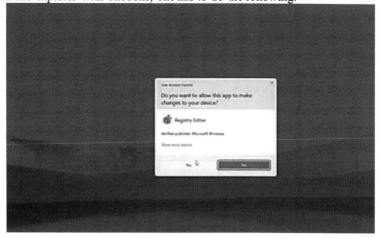

1. Click on *Windows*
2. Go to *search* and type *registry*
3. Click *ok*

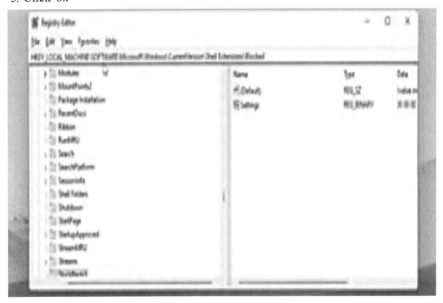

The above page will appear and the user should go to the *block key*.
4. Right click on the *block key* and select the *extreme valued option*.
5. Close the *registry*
6. Restart the *computer*

How to Open the Folder Option in Windows 11

To open and make changes to your folder;

- Press **Window + E.** This will take you to file explorer.

- Click on the options icon (…) labelled **see more.**

- Click **options.**

- You can then proceed to make changes to your folders from this page.
- Safe mode from login page
- If you're starting your PC and you want to go to safe mode directly withoutlogging in;
- From the login screen, click the power button at the bottom right.
- Press and hold the shift key and click *restart*.
- *Click on* troubleshoot > advanced options > startup settings > restart *and proceed to select a safe mode option.*

Removing Administrator Using Command Prompt

1. Reboot the PC three times to access automatic repair.
2. Click on *advanced options*
3. Click on *troubleshoot*
4. Reset your computer
5. Click on *advanced option*
6. Click on *startup repair*
7. Click on *command prompt*
   At this stage booting begins
8. Click on *accessibility icon* and the CMD will open
9. Select *user* and click on *reset password*
10. Enter the new password and apply the changes

Removing a setting from a quick setting, to do this, the user should do the following:

1. Select the *Start* button
2. Go to *Settings*.
3. Go to *System > Notifications*.
   The user can either turn notifications, banners, and sounds on or off for some or all notification senders or turn tips and suggestions about Windows *On* or *Off.*

Adding and Removing Quick Settings In Windows

To do these follow the following steps:

1. Click on the *settings*
2. Click on the *edit quick settings* using a pencil icon
3. Click on the *unpin button* you want to remove
   It can also be rearranged after the removal using the dragon—drop.

How to Change Administrator through the Control Panel

Another method to change a standard user account to the administrator account is via Control Panel. To do this, follow the steps below:

44

Step 1: Type ***Control Panel*** in the search space (search bar) at the bottom of the screen and view it in ***Category*** mode.

Step 2: ***Locate*** User Accounts ***and open.***

Step 3: Then click on ***Change account***

type

Step 3: A new window will appear with user accounts. Click on the desired user account and click on ***Change the account type.***

Step 4: Tick the ***Administrator*** box and click ***Change Account Type***.

To change back to ***Standard,*** follow the same steps above in this same way.

How to Change Administrator Using the Command Prompt

In Windows 11, to use Command Prompt to change administrator, follow the steps below: *Step 1:* With an Administrator account, run Command Prompt.

Do this by pressing ***Windows key + S*** on your keyboard and ***Windows Search*** will be launched. Type ***cmd*** in the space where ***Type here to search*** is. Then, click on ***Run as administrator*** on the right-hand side.

Step 2: Type ***net user*** and press ***Enter*** to bring out the list of users on your PC. Make note of the name of the user you want to make changes to. Let's assume it's ***Nick,*** so we note it

Step 3: Afterwards, execute the command ***net localgroup Administrators Nick /add.***

Nick in that command is the name of the user we want to change to an administrator account. On your PC, you will change Nick to the user you desire to change.

If you desire to change the user back to Standard user account type in the command ***net localgroup Administrators Nick /delete***

How to Remove a Setting from Quick Settings

In Windows 11, the Quick Settings now replace Action Center. The Quick Settings are similar to the Control Center in Mac computers.

The Quick Settings will enable user quick access settings, so that changes can be made, though it has few settings options. They are a set of status icons on the taskbar such as the Wi-Fi icon, the volume icon, and the battery icon. It can be found on the right section of the taskbar in Windows 11.

To remove a setting from Quick Settings, follow the steps below:

Step 1: A keyboard shortcut to open Quick Settings is ***Windows key + A.***

Step 2: You will see an ***icon*** similar to a ***pen***, click on it.

Step 3: The settings here will turn grey and you will see an ***unpin icon*** at the top-right corner of each setting. Click on the ***unpin icon*** to remove a setting from the Quick Settings.

Step 4: Click on ***Done*** to save changes.

Quick Settings: Adding or Removing The main purpose of Quick Settings is quick access to the settings needed as desired by the User, which can be edited as required.

To add a setting to Quick Settings in Windows 11, follow the steps below:

Step 1: Press *Windows key* + *A* key to open the Quick Settings.

Step 2: Click on the *pen icon* located at the bottom right.

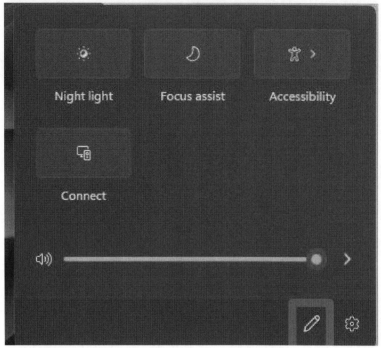

Step 3: Click *Add*.

Step 4: select the options you want added to the Quick Settings. On a PC, there are more options after accomplishing Step 3 above. They are *Nearby sharing* and *Mobile hotspot.*

Step 5: Click on *Done* to save.

How to Work with Programs, Files and Apps in Windows 11

How to Open and Manage Applications

If you want to open an application from the Start menu, click on the start menu and pick the application under All apps. If the application is also listed on the desktop and you want to launch it, you'd have to double click instead of single-clicking, which will perform the same functions.

One of the features of the Windows 11 application is on the top right.

Now on a macbook or in a macOS, those controls would be on the left-hand side. You can minimize the Apps by clicking on the little minus icon on the left, bringing the app down to the taskbar. You can preview or relaunch it by clicking on the app again. The other option is the maximize option. What you see as a partition on your screen is the new feature in Windows 11.

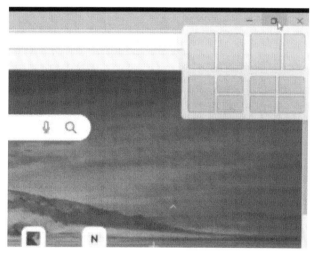

Now, this allows you with the emergence of larger desktops. Hold the mouse on the maximize icon and then select the partition to park the application in half of your screen or a certain position of your screen. So if you want to adjust, click on maximize and move down to the corner of the screen. It gives you the option for a different display split part of the screen. Then you can have something else like files or Apps on a different part of the screen. So that's another option where you can adjust the display depending on what you want. To close the application, you can click on the x icon on the top right, which is standard with other versions of Windows.

How to Use the Taskbar Manager

In some cases, when you're working on an application, and it crashes on you, you need to somehow make sure to close it without rebooting the computer. One of the ways to do that is to access or close the application from the taskbar. So let's say the application is on the taskbar, and somehow it's misbehaving. Now you need to get to the taskbar to close it.

To access a taskbar, right-click on the Windows icon and click on task manager, or you can go to the search option and type task manager. Now this will show up the task manager and the Apps you currently opened.

So if you want to end the application forcefully, click on the application and choose End task. In some cases, the application may not show up in the list. Then, in that case, click on more details and find the application, and choose End task. To find the application, click on processes.

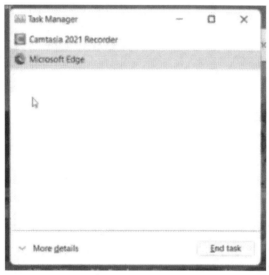

How to Switch to Different Apps In Windows 11

So in this section, we will go over how to switch between applications in Windows 11. The process is very much the same as previous versions of Windows, but to understand how the Windows 11 operating system works, we'll cover it in this book. So let's say you have two or more applications opened, and you need to switch between them with one monitor. Let's say you wanted to switch to Word. One of the options is to go to the taskbar at the bottom, click on Word to switch between the two Applications.

If you have more than two applications opened, the process will be very much the same, so you'd go to the taskbar and switch between the applications on the bottom. Another way to switch between applications is to press and hold down the **Alt key** on the keyboard and then press the **Tab key**.

That will display all the applications running currently on your computer, and at that point, you can keep on pressing the tab and switch to a different application, or while holding the **Alt key**, you can go and click on a specific one to switch to it.

How to Use Window Search

Now we are going briefly to explain how to use Windows search. Windows search is one of the cool and powerful features of the upgraded Windows operating system. Instead of having to scroll and locate various applications and identify where they are, you can click on Search and start typing for the app. That will search for Apps and all the components on the computer. It will search for documents, web, people, photos, videos, and so on.

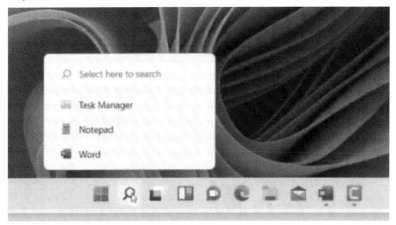

How to Customize Search Options

The search options can be customized by clicking on the three dots or options icon on the far right. Then you can customize various icons and also customize their search settings as well.

49

You can launch a search directly by clicking on the Windows icon, or you can press the Windows key and then start typing. So you can type the application's name on the search bar, click on it, and it will bring it up. You can also search for settings on your computer. When it comes up, you can change the display settings, go to the display area or any display components, and change the various settings like the scaling.

Windows Explorer and Management

Now we will go over some of the features of Windows Explorer and Windows file management. Some of these concepts may be very basic to you but are key in understanding how the operating system works and how to use Windows 11 effectively in the workplace. Think of file explorer as a mechanism to access the files you have created on your computer or the files from the various applications.

To access file explorer, click on the file explorer on your taskbar.

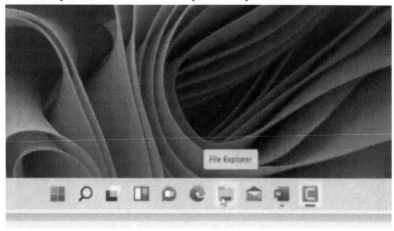

At the top, you have some of the common functions such as copy -paste and so on. Notice that those icons look slightly different. Then you have the view options whether you want to view the items as a list or whether you want to view them in large icons and so on. Then you have additional settings under the configuration option on the top right. By default, it will open at quick access. Quick access is going to give you the recent files and folders that you have accessed most recently.

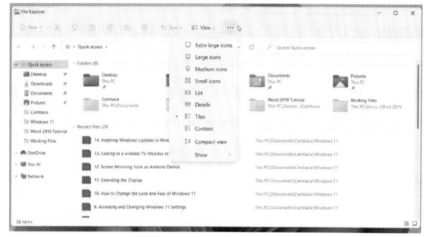

On the far right top of your file explorer, you can search for whatever is displayed in the bottom area. Below the quick access, you have the desktop option. The desktop will display any items or folders you have created or added to the desktop. So if you create a folder or a file on the desktop, that's where the icons or the items will show up.

Downloads are things that you have downloaded from the web and various browser documents. These are work documents that are stored on your computer. Now you need to understand that pictures, documents, and so on are components of your Windows account or Windows profile.

If you have multiple users that log into your computer, each user would have their separate desktop, separate documents area, and separate pictures area. The way you find that is by going under the PC. Then on the C drive where the files are stored. Go to users, and you can see all the different users on that computer.

So if you go to any of the accounts, you will notice that you have desktop, document s, downloads, and they are a replica of what's displayed on the left -hand side. So they are actually on the left-hand side, just a shortcut to what you see on the right-hand side.

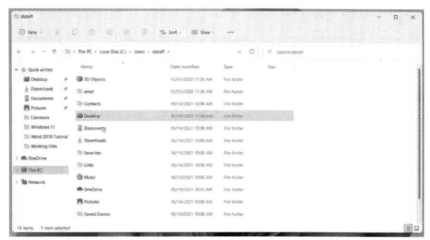

If you go to the PC, it will display the drives that exist on that PC. Also, if you are working on a network, you'd see the network drive. The Network drives typically will be mapped in particular letters like F, K, J, or M drive, or it depends on how the system administrators have set them up. That is how you access your storage on your PC and then the files within the PC. Typically the options on the quick access like the first four files are by default on your PC.

How to Remove Unwanted Applications from Your Computer

When you buy even a new computer, there might be applications you don't want, and you want to speed up the computer and remove them. You get to see what applications are installed on the computer, and you can access them a couple of ways. Go to the search option, just type Apps. Click on add and remove programs. It will list all the various programs that are installed on your computer.

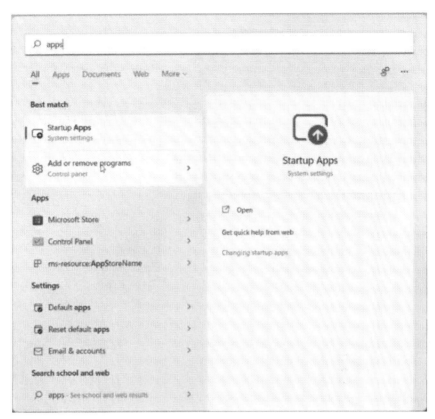

To remove any of those programs, go to any apps and click on the three dots. Then you can choose to modify it or uninstall it. When you modify, it will select new parameters for the install or reinstallation of the application.

How to Adjust the Sound Settings and Sound Volume

For some reason, this function has become more complicated in this version of Windows. You will go to the far right corner of your windows in the past and change the sound. But now, when you click on that icon for sound and volume, notice it brings you to the action center.

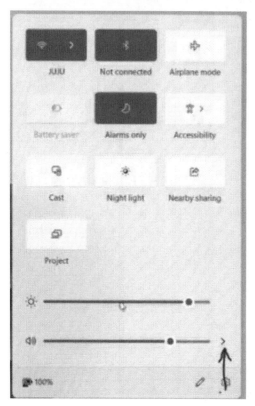

In the action center, one of the options is the sound. So if you click on the little arrow on the far right, you can change which speakers to use. There are additional settings that you can adjust as far as the sound goes. You can also get to the settings by going on the search menu and type-in sound settings.

One other option for getting to your sound setting is to move the mouse t o the sound icon and right-click. Select to open the volume mixer or the sound settings. The major change is that when you click on it, then it controls the sound from there through the action center

How to Use a Task Manager to Troubleshoot

Task managers used to be part of the taskbar in the past. So when you right-click on the taskbar, there would be an option for task manager. However, that's no longer available. You can access a task manager by simply searching on the start menu or Windows search.

There are a couple of other ways to get to the task manager. If you right -click on the Start menu, there is also the option to click on task manager, and it will take you typically to the task manager for the first time unless you change it. So it will list t he applications that are running on your computer. However, if you want additional details like what's running in the system and the processing that is taking place, and so on, then click on more details, and you'll see the processes currently running on t he PC.

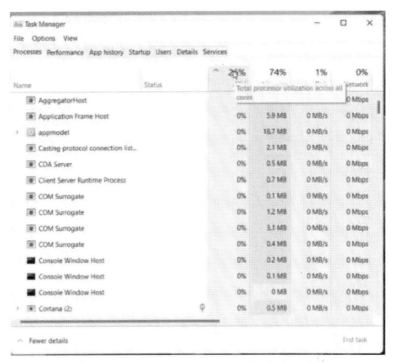

At times if the PC is running, the fans are running loud, there is typically an issue with the PC, or there is one of the applications in the computer that you need to stop. To identify which application is causing that issue, scroll up to the CPU and click the CPU utilization %. You can sort the files from highest to lowest.

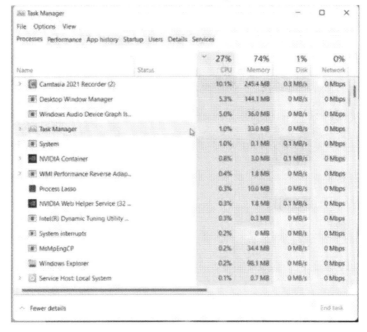

So if there is something that you need to close, click on it and then click on End Task, which will close the process. In some cases, it may not be the CPU slowing down your system. It might be certain apps that are taking most of the memory. So you can do the same thing with the memory to identify what's taking most of the memory in your computer.

When the disk utilization it's struggling, that's how you can identify that y ou have a problem with the speed of your disk. You can also identify how the processor or different components are doing over a while. So when you click on CPU, you'd be able to identify the usage under the memory usage, the solid-state drives, the drives wi-fi, graphics card, _etc_.

How to Manage Disk Storage on Windows 11

Windows 11 has a better and simpler disk management in the Windows Settings. Take the following steps to manage the disk and drive storage settings:

Step 1: *Press down the* Windows + I *keys to open the* Settings *page or open Settings from the Start Menu by clicking* Start *on the taskbar.*

Step 2: Then select *System.*

Step 3: Afterwards, click on the *Storage* settings on the left.

Step 4: *Then click on* Advanced Storage setting.

Step 5: On the right-hand pane, move down and locate *Disk & volumes*. Click on it so that you can analyze the storage device, which will show you all the devices on your PC.

Step 6: Click on any of the devices you want to have access to.

Step 7: Then, click on *Explore.*

Search for Storage Details

To search for storage details, you will do the following:

Step 1: Press down the *Windows + I* keys to open the *Settings* page.

Step 2: Then select *System.*

Step 3: Afterwards, click on the *Storage* settings on the left.

Step 4: *Then click on* Advanced Storage *setting.*

Step 5: On the right-hand pane, move down and locate *Disk & volumes*. Click on it so that you can analyze the storage device, which will show you all the devices on your PC.

How to Change Your PC Name in Windows 11

Using a special name for your PC can help you easily identify and differentiate it from other devices on a network. To change the name of your PC;

- Open the start menu and go to settings.

- Click *Rename* below your computer's default name and enter a name foryour computer.

- Click *next* and proceed to restart your device to apply the changes.

- When choosing a name for your PC, do not include special characters orspaces. Also make sure to keep the name short and easy for you to identify.

How to View Drive Usage

On your Windows 11 PC, you can know how your disk space is being used and find out the files that are using most of the storage. This process is different fromchecking the memory usage which is the RAM (Random Access Memory). You can view your drive usage with the steps below:

Click on the Windows *Start* button and select *Settings*.

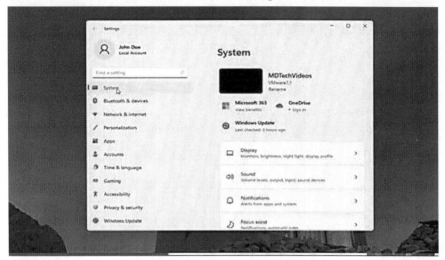

Select *System* on the left-hand side and on the right-hand side, select *Storage*. This will give you a breakdown of all your categories.

Click on *Show more*. This will give you a breakdown of your system storage usage whether it is in the System space, Apps and Features, Documents, Pictures, Music. You will see how much storage each area of your computer is using.

58

Let's say you deleted a couple of programs and you wish to check how your storage usage has improved, you can *refresh* the page to get a more accurate picture of your storage usage as well as up-to-date information about your storage usage.

Changing the Label of Your Drive

You may want to change the label of your drive on windows 11. You can do this with the use of Settings, File explorer, and Disk Management.

- Changing your label with the use of settings
- *Go to your* Windows setting.
- Click on *System* and select *Storage*.
- *Click on* Advanced storage settings *and select* Disk and Volumes.
- Next to the drive is an *arrow button* that contains the partition you want to change, click on it.
- Select the needed volume, click on *Properties.*
- Click *Change label.* Type in the *new name*, then click *Apply.*

Changing the label Using Disk Management

Click on the *Search Icon.* Type in *Disk Management* and click on it.

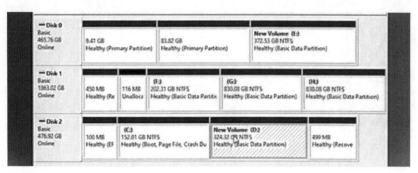

Right-click on the Volume you want to rename and select *Properties.*

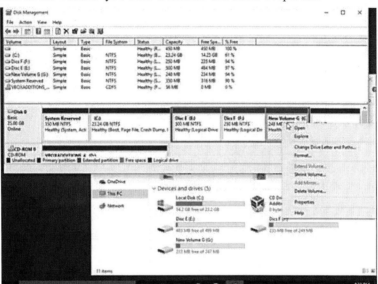

Enter the new name. Then click *Apply,* then *Ok.*

60

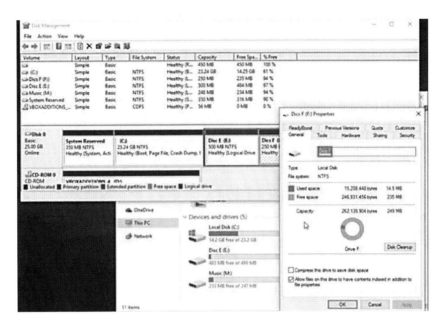

Changing the Label Using File Explorer

- Click on *File Explorer* on the Taskbar.

- Right-click on the drive you want to rename.

- Enter the name you would like to rename the drive.

- Click Apply, then Ok

Understanding Partition in Windows 11

How to Create a Partition on Windows 11

A partition is a logical separation of a hard drive. It is like turning a hard drive into two. When a partition is created, a user can have different operating systems on the same hard disk. Disk/Drive partitioning means dividing your hard drive into multiple sections and making that section available to the operating system. If you have a large hard drive, organizing your files can be made easier with disk partitioning. To create a partition, simply follow the steps listed below:

- Open the *Search* icon down in your taskbar.

- On the search box, type in *Computer Management*.

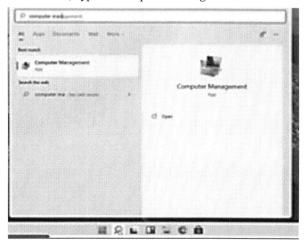

- Select *Disk Management* underneath storage and select the disk you want to partition.

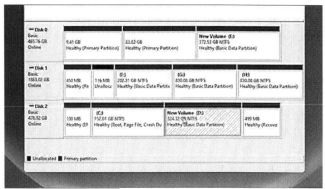

- Right-click on it, then select *Shrink Volume*.

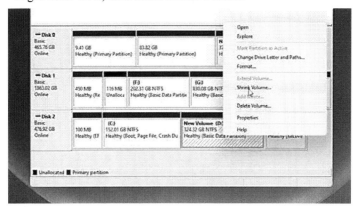

- Enter the size you want this new partition to be. Let's say 100 Megabytes. Then, select *Shrink*.

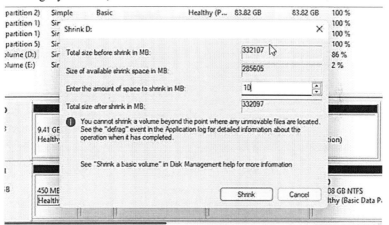

- Once that's done, you Right-click on the newly created space and select *New simple volume*.

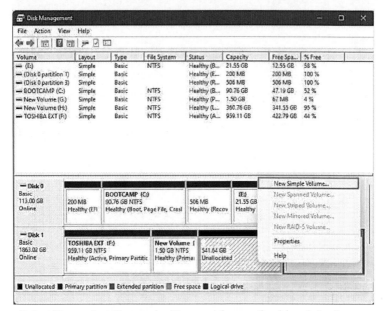

- Select *Next*, select *Next* again. You can change the drive letter here as well, as long as it is not being currently used on the computer.

- Select *Next*. You can name this created space whatever you want. Then select *Finish*.

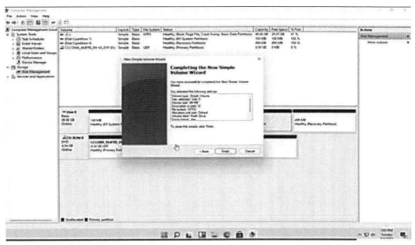

A pop-up menu will appear indicating that the drive is being recognized.

How to Extend a Partition on Windows 11

Your PC might be running out of space and would like to ext end the size of your drive, you can do this using the Disk Management tool. Follow the outlined procedure to do so;

- Click on the *Windows Start* button.

- On the Search Box, type *Disk Management.*

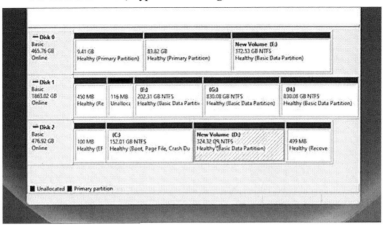

- *Right-click* on the partition you would like to extend. Note that the partition can only be extended when there is an available space after the partition you want to extend. Then, click on the *Extend Volume* option.

- The Extend Volume Wizard menu will open, select *Next.*

- Type in the size you wish to extend the partition on the *"Select the amount of space in MB"* option.

- Click the *Next* button. If the Next button is not available, it means that the value you entered is too high.

- Click on the *Finish* button.

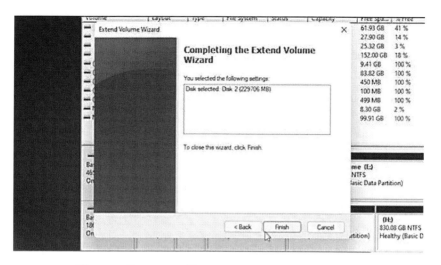

How to Increase/Decrease the Partition Size

Reducing or increasing partition drives can help you deal with disk or upgrade problems. To do this;

- Go to *settings > system > storage > advanced storage settings > disk & volumes.*

- Once the disk and volumes have been dropped down, select the drive you want to make this change on.

- Click on the partition you want to adjust and tap *properties.*

- On the next page, click *change size.*

- You can proceed to enter your desired size. To get accurate storage sizes for your input, always multiply by 1024 (1GB). For instance if you want to input a space of 40GB, multiply 40 by 1024: 40 x 1024 = 40960.

How to Format or Delete the Partition

Files and data should be backed up before formatting the disk partition. To delete or format disk partition, do the following:

Step 1: Press down the *Windows + I* keys to open the *Settings* page or open *Settings* from the *Start Menu* by clicking *Start* on the taskbar.

Step 2: *Then click on* Advanced Storage setting.

Step 3: On the right-hand pane, move down and locate *Disk & volumes*.

Step 4: Select the drive you wish to work on. The drive's partition will be displayed.

Step 5: Click on the partition you wish to work on and click on *Properties*.

Step 6a: Locate and click on *Delete* to delete your partition. Follow the instructions afterward to finish the process.

Step 6b: However, to format the drive, only click *format* and not delete.
Depending on the size of the partition, it will take a few seconds or minutes to complete.

Using the Search and New Emojis

The touch keyboard in Windows 11 has new dedicated emojis and GIFs, which is lacking in that of Windows 10. To use, follow the steps below:

Step 1: On the Taskbar, locate and click on the *touchpad icon.*

Step 2: Click on the *emoji icon* on the left, just beside settings (gear-like) icon.

Step 3: there you will see diverse emojis and GIFs.

Step 4: Use the search bar to search for GIFs and emojis.

Step 5: There is also clipboard history, which can be used on the touch keyboard. First, click on the *emoji icon* on the left, and then at the left-hand corner, click on the *clipboard icon*. This will show the clipboard history from which you can then click on the desired text or image.

How to Use Transparency Effects

This means how visible the system is and enabling transparency effect means promoting the flow and design of the taskbar.

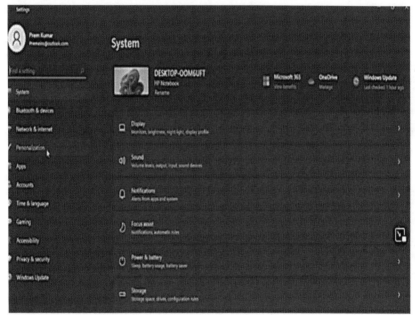

Steps to enable transparency effect:

1. Click on *setting*
2. Click on *personalization* under settings page
3. Click on *colors* under personalization
4. Click on *transparency effect* under colors.

The user needs to activate the windows to see the transparency effect if it has not been done initially.

68

Also, there is an alternative method to this

1. Open *search*
2. Search for *translucent TB.*

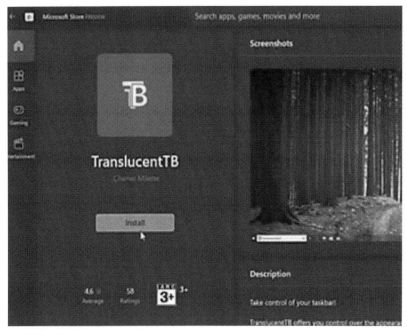

3. Click on *Install*

This app is supported by Windows 10 but not supported by Windows 11 but it will guarantee   the   user   100% transparency. The settings can also be changed by following this process.

1. Right click on the *translucent*
2. Go to *regular*
3. Under Regular, choose if you want it normal, accent color, clear, opaque, blur or fluent.

The new Windows 11 touch keyboard has an option to use emoji, unlike Windows 10. It also has options to use transparency effect, animated GIF search bar and more.

The transparent effect of the touch keyboard in Windows 11 is a feature that makes the touch keyboard look somewhat transparent. Nevertheless, the keyboard has to be docked. By default, it is docked at the lower end of the screen.

To undock, there is an undocking button on the right-hand corner of the touch keyboard, click on it. This will enable you to move the touch keyboard aro und, as you like. To dock the keyboard back, click on the same button.

The taskbar also appears transparent, having shades of the colourful background used for desktop. This is a default setting.

In the section, however, we shall look at how to disable it, if so desired.

Disable Windows 11's Transparency Effects

In Windows 11, there are two methods of disabling the transparency feature—through Personalization Settings and through Accessibility Settings.

To disable transparency effects through Personalization, follow these steps:

Step 1: Get to *Personalization* through Settings or right-click on the desktop and click on *Personalize*.

Step 2: On Personalization settings, click on *Colors*.

Step 3: Thereafter, turn off the *Transparency effects switch* and it will be disabled.

Next, we shall look at the other method. To disable transparency effects through Accessibility Settings, follow these steps:

Step 1: Press the *Windows key + I* to open the settings app.

Step 2: Then click *Accessibility* on the left side of the Settings window.

Step 3: In the Accessibility options, click on the *virtual effects* tab. This will bring up all the settings of effect used in the Windows user interface.

Step 4: Look for *Transparency effects* and turn off the Transparency effects button.

How to Use the Keyboard in Windows 11

How to Customize Touch Keyboard in Windows 11

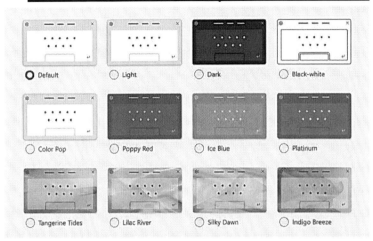

In windows 11, you can customize your keyboard by changing the theme, wallpaper, key text size and background and keyboard size.

To change the size and theme of your touch keyboard:

- Go to settings.

- Click on *personalization.*

- *Tap* touch keyboard.

- You'll be introduced to a page full of *keyboard themes.* Click on a theme to enable it as your keyboard theme.

- On top of the page is the *keyboard size.* Use the slider to increase or decrease the keyboard size. You can also choose to use a floating touch keyboard which you can position anywhere on the screen. To do this, click on the first icon or docking button located at the top left side of the keyboard when it is open.

How to Change Keyboard Settings

- Click on the search icon from the taskbar.

- Type *control panel* into the search field and click on the corresponding result.

- Set *view by* to large icons and click *keyboard.*

- On the next pop up, you'll see the keyboard properties. You can adjust the repeat delay and also change the repeat rate as well. Also use the slider to change the cursor blink rate.

Using Handwriting and Various Keyboard Layouts

With the new touch keyboard, you can also use different layouts for more diversit y. You also have the option to write with your handwriting and have it converted into text on your PC.

To use a different keyboard layout;

- Open keyboard and click on the settings icon at the top left side.

- Tap the *keyboard* option.

- You can then proceed to select from default, small or split layouts for your keyboard.

- Click on *Handwriting* to enable the feature for your writing. This means that you can make your text inputs using your handwriting, which will then be converted into computer texts.

How to Use the Search

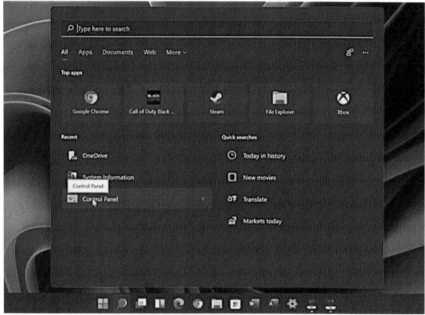

The search feature is the second on the start bar. With this feature, you can easily search for items on our system.

Click on the search icon to open and click on the search field to input your search words. On the pop up search menu, you'll find the recently opened apps and control panel below.

How to Use Clipboard Paste as Text

In Windows 11, copied items in their original forms can be pasted and then modified to plain text.

Step 1: Open a desired file in text format.

Step 2: Then, press down the ***Windows*** *+ V* keys on the keypad to open the history tab of the Clipboard.

Step 3: Then, click on ***the three-dots*** just beside the copied text, and click ***Paste as text***.

What are the Different Types of Files that Can Be Stored in Clipboard?

Texts, images, scripts, links, documents and videos less than 4MB can be stored in Clipboard on Windows 11. Maximum number of items supported in the Clipboard is 25. The most recent item copied stays at the top. The oldest copied item is removed bottom up when new ones are added.

Enabling the Clipboard History in Windows 11

This section will take you to step by step through the process of enabling history in your clipboard in Windows 11. This will allow you to have multiple items saved to your clipboard at once.

- Firstly, right-click on the start button and select ***settings*** ▮▮▮▮ ***System*** onthe left side of the screen if it does not automatically take you there (as seen in the image below).

- And then, on the right side of the screen, scroll down and locate the ***clipboard.*** Go ahead and left-click on it.

- Next, underneath the ***clipboard history,*** you'll find a little switch at the side. Go ahead and toggle it on (as seen in the picture below)

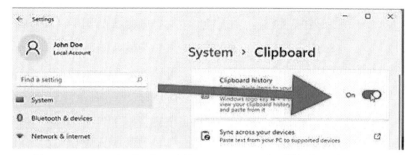

- Now, to access the keyboard history, tap on the **Windows logo** key and the *V* key at the same time to launch the clipboard history whenever you might need it. It would appear at the bottom right corner of the screen as seen in the image below.

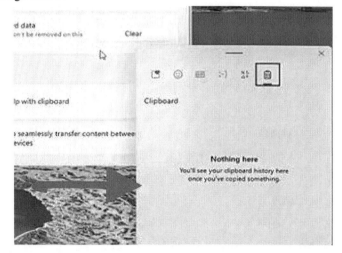

How to Use Emojis in Touch Keyboard

To enable emojis in touch keyboard;

- Open the keyboard by tapping a text field.
- Click on the icon at the left, just above the keyboard texts. You can selectbetween different emojis and also Gifs.

How to Use Voice Typing in Touch Keyboard

Voice typing now makes your writing much easier. To use this feature;

- Enter a text field on your PC.
- Press **Windows + H** on your keyboard and proceed to say your sentences.
- Click on the settings icon on the voice typing pop up to make some adjustments to voice typing.
- In voice typing settings, you can enable or disable auto punctuation to give you more flexibility.

What to Do If Search Stops Working

Sometimes, the search feature might experience little glitches that might prevent it from opening. To fix this problem;

Step 1: Restart your PC

- Since the Windows 11 software is still undergoing its update process, you have to understand that your PC might experience some bugs with the beta version.
- Right-click the start icon and select **shut down or sign out** and then click **restart.**

Step 2: Use the command prompt

- Press **WIN + R** to open the run dialog box then close it again. Sometimes, this might fix the problem.

Step 3: Troubleshooter

- You can use the troubleshooter option to fix the search problem. Go tosettings from the start menu.
- *Click* Update & security.
- Tap *troubleshoot.*
- *Click on* additional troubleshooters.
- *Click* search and indexing.
- Tap *Run the troubleshooter* and proceed with the next instructions.

Step 4: Enable the search button

- Your search button may not be enabled on the taskbar and that may be thecause of the problem.
- To make sure the search button is enabled, right-click the start icon and click *settings.*
- Click *personalization* and click on *taskbar.*
- On the taskbar page, turn the search feature on by tapping the toggle.

Step 5: Check the search service

- *Press* Windows + R *on your keyboard to launch the* run *feature*.
- Type in *services.msc* and press enter to go to the location.
- Check for the *Windows search* service. If it displays *running* on the statuscolumn, right-click and tap restart. Check if the issue has been fixed.
- If the status column for the windows-search-service is blank, right-click onit and click *Properties.*
- Under properties, click the Startup type drop down and select *Automatic.*
- Tap *start* and click *ok* to apply the changes.

How to Use Several Keyboard Layouts

In Windows 11, the user interface of the touch keyboard makes the keyboard layout very easy to use. Do the following to make use of the keyboard layout:

Step 1: Locate on the taskbar, the touch keyboard button and click on it.

Step 2: From the screen that appears, click on the gear icon on the left-hand corner. The gear icon represents settings.

Step 3: Click on the *Keyboard layout>,* then you will have access to the different keyboard layouts—default, small, split and handwriting tool, as well.

The default keyboard layout completely covers the lower part of the screen that comes up when you open the touch keyboard. The small is a smaller size of the touch keyboard. While the split divided the screen into two to enable you type with both hands. For the Handwriting tool, do the following to enable it:

Step 1: Click on the gear icon (settings) on the left-hand corner of the touch-keyboard screen.

Step 2: Then, click on ***Handwriting***.

This feature allows you to write texts with your handwriting, which Windows 11 will recognize and convert to words in des ired fonts.

Changing the Keyboard Layout

- Firstly, you can right-click on your Windows icon, and click on the ***settings***

This will open up the settings window and at the left side of the screen, tap on ***time and language.***

- When ***time and language*** open up, next, click on the ***language and region*** section as seen in the image below.

- The next window that will show will display languages that are supported by your Windows 11 computer OS. As seen in the image below, there is only one language set as the default language which is English (UK).

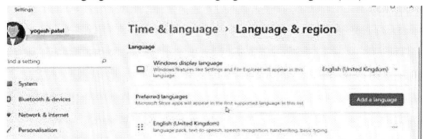

- To change the keyboard language layout, you can select from the array of available languages, but first, they must be added to the layout for them to function.

Adding a Keyboard Layout

To add a language, follow step by step the instructions in the subtopic above (*Changing the keyboard layout*).

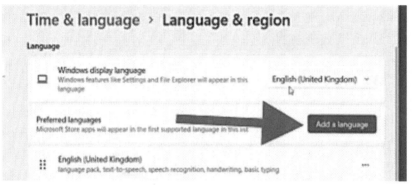

Next, click on the *add language* button.

Removing a Keyboard Layout

- The first step is to run this command- *$1=New-WinUserLanguageList en-US*

- Then, type in *power shell* in the windows search box and make a right-click on windows power cell and then click on *run as an administrator.*

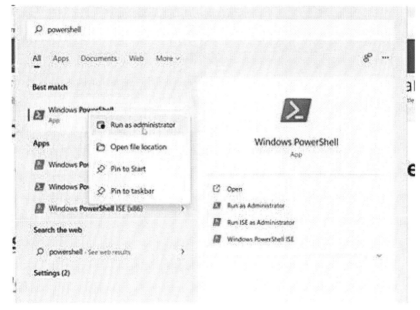

Select power shell as an administrator and click on yes.

- Paste the command in step one
- Then, hit the *enter* key
- When that is done, go ahead and run this command— *Set-WinUserLanguageList $1*
- Paste it and hit the enter key
- Once you back to *settings >language and region,* you will find that all the other languages are gone except the default language.

How to Activate Input Indicator

- Right-click on the start button
- Select *settings*
- Select *Bluetooth and devices* on the left side of the screen

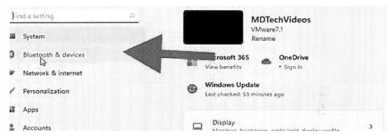

- Then on the right side, locate the *mouse* and left-click on that.

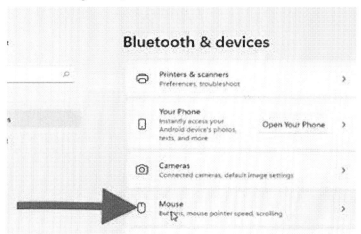

On the mouse menu, go all the way down and locate the *mouse pointer*

- Scroll down again and select *text cursor*
- In that menu, you will find a *text cursor indicator.* Toggle it on

79

Understanding the Taskbar in Windows 11

There are many ways you can completely customize your taskbar on Windows 11. Customizing your taskbar means changing the default looks of your taskbar. We will guide you on how to do so. We will look at some of the basics like how to pin and unpin apps on the taskbar, how to change the color of your taskbar, how to remove the default icons on the taskbar etc. So, let's get started.

How to Pin and Unpin Apps on the Taskbar

Click on the *Search icon* and type in the app you want to pin.

Right-click on it. Then, select *Pin to Taskbar*.

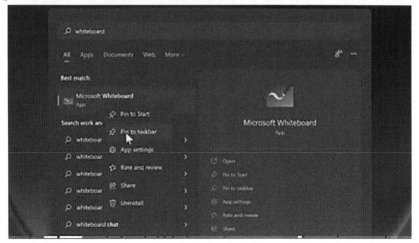

You can also pin a running application. Just open an application and when it is open, you will see the app's icon on the taskbar. Right-click on it and select *Pin to Taskbar*.

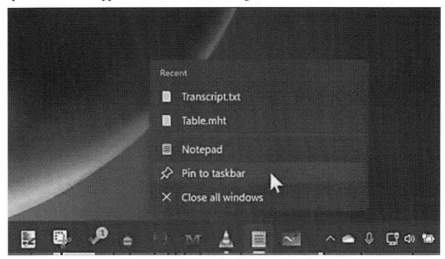

To unpin an app from the taskbar, simply; *Right-click* on the app icon on your taskbar. Then, select *Unpin from taskbar*.

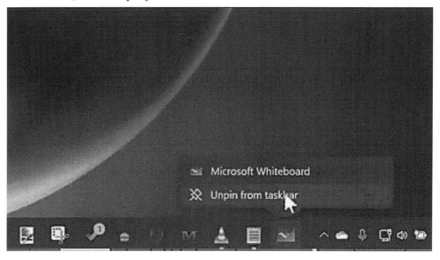

Quick Settings

This is one of the features of Windows 11. On Windows 10, it was a part of the Action Center. The Quick Settings menu is where you manage common PC settings easily and quickly, like *Volume, Bluetooth, Wi-Fi, Brightness.* You can also find Media playback controls that appear when you play music with Microsoft Edge. You may want to make a setting to your computer but you don't want to go through the settings application, the Quick Settings flyout can help you make that setting faster.

The Quick Settings flyout is located at the lower right-hand side of the taskbar. To open Quick Settings on Windows 11 you are to press *The Windows key + A* on the keyboard. You can also open the Quick Settings flyout by clicking on the *Quick Settings area* on the taskbar, as shown on the image below;

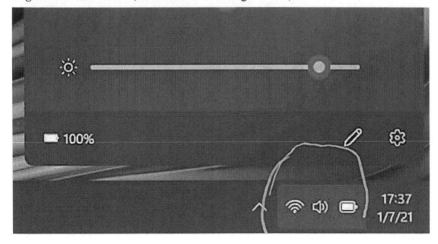

How to Customize Your Quick Settings Flyout

You can customize your Quick Settings by adding or removing a setting from the Quick Settings menu.

To add a setting to your Quick Settings, simply follow the steps below;

- *Press the* Windows key + A *to open the* Quick Settings panel.

- Click on the *Pencil icon* at the lower right-hand side of the prompt.

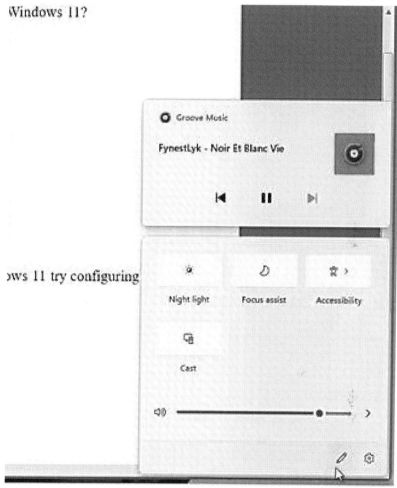

- Select *Add.* Then, select the *Settings* you wish to add to Quick Settings.

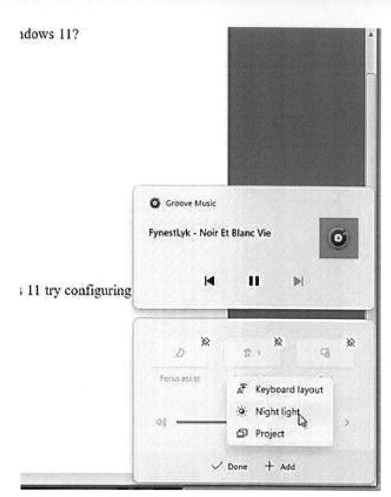

; 11 try configuring

- Click *Done* to finish and save changes.
- To remove a setting from Quick Settings all you have to do is:
- *Press the* Windows key + A *to open* Quick Settings.
- Click on the *Pencil icon.*
- Click on the *Unpin icon* on the top-right corner of the setting you want to remove.

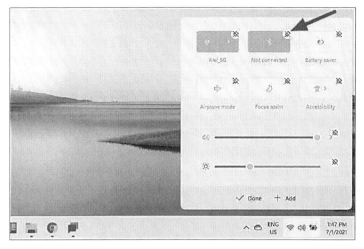

- Click on *Done* to save changes.

How to Move Taskbar to the Top of the Screen

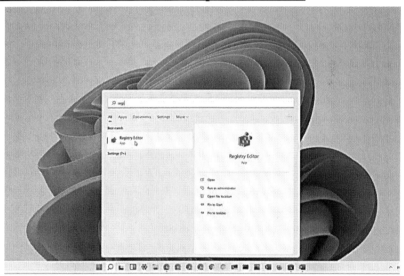

If you want to change the position of your taskbar from the bottom to the top of your screen you might have to go through a tedious and risky process. This process involves editing the registry, which is a very risky thing to do. You should only do this if you are sure of not making a mistake, which could result in a serious problem. Also, make sure to backup your computer before making this change in case you need to recover any altered document.

To begin;

- Go to the start menu and search for the registry editor.
- Click on the corresponding result to open the registry editor.

85

- Go to the following path
  HKEY_CURRENT_USER\Softwa re\Microsoft\Windows\CurrentVersion\
  Explorer\StuckRects3

- This will bring you to a folder containing *settings.*

- Double tap the *settings* option to open its attributes.

- Select the first number (03) under the *FE* column. Make sure the cursor isplaced in front of the number.

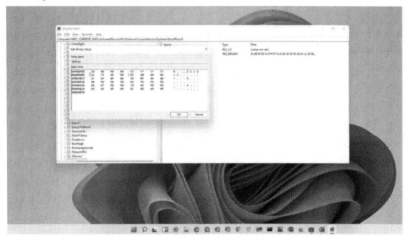

- Delete once and type in 01 then click *OK* to apply the change.

- After this, right-click on the start icon and click *task manager.*

- Scroll down to the *Windows explorer* process and click it.

- Click *restart,* to restart windows explorer.

Once this is done, your taskbar will be displayed at the top of your screen.

To return the taskbar to its original position follow the same steps above;

- When you get to the folder containing the settings option, double tap the *settings* to open up its content.

- Delete the *01* value under the same *FE* column and type in *03*.

- Click *OK* to apply the change.

- Go to task manager and restart the *Windows explorer* again. You'll have your taskbar at the bottom of the screen again.

How to Perform a System Restore in Windows 11

Sometimes, the updates may not be favorable. System restore can help you go back to a point in your Window's time where it was good enough for you.

To do this;

- On your keyboard, press *Windows + R.* This will open the run window.

- Type in *sysdm.cpl* and tap *Ok.* This command will bring up a *system protection* pop up page.

- Click on system Protection.

- Tap systemrestore below.

- When the systemrestore page opens up, Click *next.*

- To see a list of programs that will be reversed after the restoration, click *scan for affected programs.*

- Select a restore point and tap *next* to continue

- Click *finish* to conclude to begin the restore process.

How to Personalize the Taskbar in Windows 11

So, it turns out that personalizing the Windows 11 taskbar isn't as difficult as you may assume. Continue reading for more knowledge that will make you into a master in operating Windows 11.

How to Tie an Application to the Taskbar in Windows 11

- Uninstall pinned programs and items from the taskbar in Windows 11.

- Shift the items on the taskbar to the left.

- In Windows 11, you may choose to hide or reveal the taskbar corner symbols.

87

Multiple Desktop

The next icon on the taskbar represents the multiple Windows feature. This lets you create multiple windows on your PC. You can create these new windows with different backgrounds and easily switch between them. Click on the multiple desktop feature and tap the pop up with the + icon to create a new desktop.

To change the background or rename your desktop;

- Click on the desktop icon to display your different desktops.

- Touch and hold a desktop to display its options.

- Click on *change background* or *rename* and proceed to make the adjustment.

How to Attach an Application to the Taskbar in Windows 11

Yes, you can still pin programs to the taskbar in Windows 11, and there are a few different ways to do so. Like you've rightfully guessed, we'll talk about how to accomplish this in the simplest possible manner, so let's get started.

Choose a Running Application to Pin

When you start an application, it will display on your system's taskbar with a logo and a line beneath it indicating that it's running. If you wish to attach the program to your system's taskbar, just right-click on it and choose Pin to taskbar.

Pin an Application that Isn't Executing

In a scenario where the application isn't operating, but its icon is situated on the Desktop, all you've got to do now is right-click on the logo then pick Show more preference. To make it display on the redesigned taskbar in Windows 11, select Pin to the taskbar that's available at the context menu.

Pin Applications from the Start Menu

- To access applications in the Start Menu, hit the Windows button on yourcomputer or select the Start button from the taskbar.

- Select All Applications from there, then locate the application you'd like to pin.

- Lastly, right-click on the program and choose More > Pin to Taskbar fromthe menu.

Widgets Icon

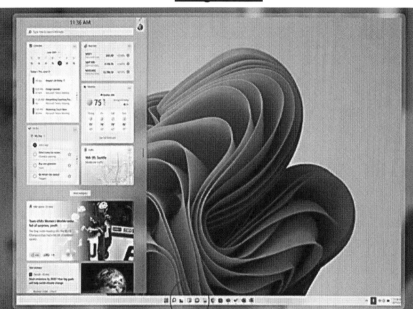

You can now view your important updates using this feature. You'll find the weather, news and calendar widget. You can also add new widgets as well for more diversity. To do this;

- Click on the widget icon, which is the fourth icon on the taskbar. This willopen up a widget panel on the left side.

- You can also bring up the widget by swiping from the left side on touch screen laptops. To make it go away, simply tap on the screen.

- Click *Add widgets* and select a new widget.

- You can also customize the size of a widget by clicking the options icon at the top right side of the widget box. Choose between *small, medium or large* sizes for your widget.

- To remove a widget, click the options icon at the top right side of the widget box and tap *remove widget.*

89

- The search field at the top of the widget page can also be used to search the web.

New Family and Entertainment Widgets

Family Widget The Windows 11 also introduces a new family widget to your widget menu. With this new widget, you can see the activities of the members included in your family groups online. If you have family groups setup on your Microsoft account, this feature can be very useful to you.

If this feature is not included in the widget menu by default, you can always add it. To do this;

- Click *Add widget* from the widget menu and select *family safety.*

- To remove the widget, simply click on the options button (…) at the top right corner of the widget and click *remove widget.*

Entertainment Widget A new entertainment widget has also been added to the widget menu. On this widget, you'll see the latest movies from the Microsoft store. You can scroll through the movies using the arrows at the side of the widget. Click on a movie you find interesting and you'll be directed to the movie on Microsoft store.

This feature is not enabled by default so you'll have to enable it manually. To do this;

- Click *Add widget* from the widget menu.

- Scroll through the widget options and select *entertainment.*

- Follow the steps above to remove the widget.

Eliminate Pinned Programs and Items from the Taskbar in Windows 11

After you've added a few programs, you might need to delete some of them from the Windows 11 taskbar to ensure that the numbers are down. This is an easy task. Hence, let's talk about how to complete it efficiently.

Unpin applications through the taskbar:

- To do so, right-click on the app's icon and select Properties.

- Then choose Unpin from Taskbar from the drop-down menu.

- The symbol should go right away unless you wish it to reappear.

Unpin applications through the taskbar Settings section:

- Another option for removing programs is to go to the taskbar configuration.

- To do so, hold down the Windows + I to bring up the Settings menu.

- Alternatively, pick Settings from the fastened applications area by pressing the Start Menu option.

- Next, navigate to Personalization > Taskbar.

- Then click the toggle option to remove programs and symbols from the taskbar in Windows 11.

Shift the Taskbar Items to the Left from the Center to the Left

The majority of users are accustomed to a taskbar with icons on the left-hand side and the Start Menu option on the furthest bottom edge. You can go back to that look if you want, and we expect a lot of Windows 11 customers to do so straight now.

- To do so, right-click on your taskbar and choose Taskbar Settings.

- A popup screen will spring up with a variety of alternatives to pick from.

- Change the Taskbar Behavior to Left from Center by scrolling down to Taskbar Behavior.

You should also be able to automatically conceal the taskbar, display badges on programs, and conceal the right-hand far corner option that displays the Desktop.

How Do I Hide or Show Taskbar corner symbols in Windows 11?

The icons that display in the status area of the taskbar are called taskbar corner icons.

- Go to the Taskbar Settings section.

- To append or delete the Virtual Touchpad, Touch Keyboard, or Pen Menugo to the Taskbar corner icons.

Overflow and Taskbar Corner Icons

The taskbar corner icons are the symbols on the taskbar's right-hand corner that display information like the date and time, Wi-Fi status, volume level, and battery level, among other items. When you pick the arrowhead to the left -hand side of those side symbols, the overflow displays as a little display menu.

The symbols in the overflow pane are primarily intended to alert you whenever you have to do something, such as texts that have come or an upgrade that is required. This is especially useful for programs that run concurrently, such as Discord; you can simply shut them off from the overlay by right-clicking on their symbol and selecting "quit."

While the majority of the Windows side symbols are fixed, some, such as the Virtual touchpad, Touch keyboard, and Pen Menu may be concealed. They're accessible via the very same taskbar options menu that allows us to relocate items to the left-hand side; simply choose "Taskbar corner icons" and turn off the items you wouldn't like to view.

Ungrouping Icons in the Taskbar in Windows 11

To stop the clustering of items on your Windows 11 taskbar, stick to the following steps. This solution will need you to download classic taskbar skins that turn your Windows 11 computer's taskbar to resemble a Windows 10 taskbar.

Unfortunately, if you don't want to modify the appearance of the taskbar, this solution will not function for you. This is presently the only option to deactivate icon clustering in the Windows 11 taskbar. To start, stick to the following steps.

Step-by-Step Instructions

Download Winaero Tweaker and prepare to install it on a Windows 11 computer first. Execute the.exe file after unzipping the package. Next, to install the application on your computer, complete the following on-screen directions.

After installing the software, go to the left and pick 'Classic Start Menu and Taskbar.'

'Enable Classic Taskbar and Start Menu' should be checked.

You can either reboot your computer or log out and back into an existing Windows account. The taskbar at the base of the display should have been updated after you've authenticated back in. Unfortunately, the Windows symbol for the Start Menu is no more functional, and fast setup symbols for WiFi, volume and other options are no more visible on your display. Let's get things straightened up. Type the command below by pressing Windows + R.

SystemIcons

To perform your request, hit 'Enter' on the keyboard or hit 'Ok' on the mouse. You'll now be presented with a box where you may choose which system symbols you want to see in the taskbar. At the base of the display, select 'Turn systemicons off or on.'

Select the items you want to see on the taskbar and turn them on.

After you've activated all of the essential icons, run the.exe for 'Classic Start' that we installed previously. To run Classic Start on your Computer, complete the on -screen prompts.

Your computer's Start menu key must now function properly. Try clicking and using the fresh Start Menu to see how it works. We're now prepared to deactivate icon clustering on your computer. Look for PowerShell in the start menu. When the application appears in the search queries, select it to open it. To run the command, paste it into your PowerShell and hit the Enter button.

REG   ADD
"HKCU\Software\Microsoft\Windows\CurrentVersion\Explorer\Advanced   "   v
TaskbarGlomLevel t REG DWORD /d 2

Reboot your computer immediately.

Customer reviews

I would be incredibly thankful if you could take just 60 seconds to write a brief review on Amazon, even if it's just a few sentences!

Add an App to Taskbar

The taskbar is the quickest way to get to your most used apps. To add an app to this quick access location;

- Click on the Windows icon to go to the start menu.
- Locate the app to add to your taskbar. Click *all apps* for more options in caseyou can't find the app on the first page.
- Once located, right-click on the app and tap *pin to taskbar.*
- On other occasions, you can find this option after you click on *more.*

How to Boot Your PC in Safe Mode

If you have difficulty booting your system, you can enter into safe mode and troubleshoot the PC without signing in. To do this;

- Turn on your PC and turn it off again as soon as the Windows logo appearson the screen.
- Do this two more times after which your PC will be directed into an automatic repair page.
- *Click* advanced options > troubleshoot > advanced options > Startup settings > restart *and then proceed to select a safe mode to boot into.*

How to Change Administrator on Windows 1 Using the ControlPanel

- Click on start and type *control panel* in the search field.
- Select the corresponding control panel result to proceed.
- Once in the control panel, change the view to *category.*
- Tap *change account type* under user account.
- Select the administrator option and click *change account type* to proceed. This will change the administrator account into a standard account.

How to Fix Desktop Crashes in Windows 11

Since the release of the Windows 11 beta version, many users have complained about how their software crashes frequently. If you notice that your Windows 11 PC keeps crashing, it could be a problem with the beta version you're running. The inconsistency and 'buginess' of beta versions is why many users wait for official releases of the windows updates. An update to the official version might be the lasting solution for the crashes; however, there are some steps you can apply to treat this problem now.

Step 1: Reinstall the new software

- If the software installed on your PC is corrupt, your PC might experience crashes. To be sure you have not installed the wrong software, try reinstalling the software *from the official page.*

Step 2: Uninstall old drivers Some drivers in your system may be outdated. If the crash came with a message telling you what failed, you should take note of the problem Windows is pointing to. Sometimes it could refer to the failure of audio drivers or other outdated drivers. Once you know the name of the driver, you can proceed to uninstall it.

- Go to the start menu and open *device manager*.

- Go to the category of the hardware component you wish to uninstall. Forinstance, if it is an audio driver, click on *sound, video and game controller.*

- Under the hardware section, right-click the specific driver and tap *uninstall device.*

- Tap on *allow* to remove the driver.

- Click *Uninstall* to proceed. Drivers are usually updated automatically atstartups.

- After the uninstallation, reboot your systemand see if the problem is fixed.

Step 3: Troubleshoot your PC

- The Windows troubleshooter is available to fix these types of issues. To fix the problems using troubleshooting, Click on *start* and search *troubleshoot.*

- Under the troubleshoot page, you'll find different sections. Go to a section related to your crash trigger. For instance, if your system crashed while trying to open a video, click *video playback* and follow the suggestions offered by the troubleshooter to fix the problem.

How to Go Back to Windows 10

If you think you might have made a mistake jumping into the Windows 11 beta or you find yourself wishing you had stayed on Windows 10, you can still achieve that. Most users consider this when the bugs become too much to handle. This is a reason why it's not advisable to download beta versions on your official PC. You can easily downgrade your PC back to Windows 10 while you wait for the official Windows 11 software, which will be released during the holiday season.

To begin;

- Click on the *start menu* and go to *settings.*

- At the bottom left side of the settings page, click on *Windows update.*

- Click on advanced options.

- Scroll down and click *recovery.*

- On the recovery page, click on *go back* beside the *previous version of Window* option. This will begin the Windows 10 installation process.

- When you click on the *go back* option, you'll see a page asking why you want to go back. Select the option(s) most relevant to your experience. You can as well use the text field to tell Microsoft more about why you're going back. This will help Microsoft upgrade their services to better serve you.

- Click *next* after providing the feedback.

94

- On the next page, you'll see an option to check for updates. Since there areno updates yet, click *no thanks.*
- Click *next.*
- Click *next* again.
- Click on *Go back to earlier build.* This will begin the installation of Windows 10.

To do this;

- Click on the *start menu.*
- Click on the *settings* icon.
- On the setting page, click on *update & security.*
- Click on *Windows insider program* at the bottom of the left menu.
- Under the *stop getting preview builds* option; turn the toggle on to prevent Windows from updating automatically to Windows 11.
- Restart your Windows.

How to Use Cleanup Recommendations

With Windows 11, you now have a cleanup recommendation feature. This feature gives you recommendations about files that can be deleted to free up space for your computer. These recommendations are files that will not affect your PC when deleted.

To use this feature;

- Go to settings.
- *Click* storage *and select* cleanup recommendations.
- On the cleanup recommendations page, you'll see the option to select your recycle bin and delete it to free up space.
- You'll also see a *temporary Windows installation files* option which you can also delete.
- Under the large and unused apps, you will see a list of apps you might haveno need for. You can also delete these.
- Also you will have the option to delete files that have already been synched to the cloud to free up space on your computer.
- Once you have clicked on the check boxes, proceed to delete them using the *delete* button below the selection.

Archive apps

You can archive some apps you do not use automatically using this feature. With this, you can save space and bandwidth on your PC by having the version of the app stored online for you.

To locate this feature;

- Go to settings.

- Click *apps.*
- Tap app features.
- Under more settings, click archive apps.
- You can proceed to turn this feature on to automate the process.

When an app is archived, it will be deleted from your PC but will be downloaded automatically the next time you open it.

Differences Between Windows 10 and Windows 11

Windows 11 has a number of new elements that assists users in managing multiple tasks with numerous windows and working with multiple monitors.

The quality of the updates has also improved. Updates are now made up to 40% smaller, and they will be installed in the background by Windows. Also, unlike Windows 10, Windows 11 will only receive one major upgrade per year, rather than the two that Windows 10 receives.

Microsoft has again added a widgets pane to the taskbar, as well as Microsoft Teams integration for simple talking and calling.

The Microsoft Store in Windows 11 has remarkably improved: Finally, the Store now contains any Windows app so desired. Even Android apps are now available and can be downloaded from the Store.

There are several modifications for PC gaming. Auto HDR and DirectStorage have now found their way to the PC from the Xbox Series X, enhancing graphics in classic games and reducing latency in modern games on robust PCs.

New UI and Design

The new interface design is the very first feature you'll discover when you install Windows 11. Every user interface component and the window now have curved edges, thanks to a redesign by Microsoft.

This holds for both the context menu and the File Explorer. Some people aren't delighted with this new context menu feature in Windows 11, but then you can turn it off if you wish.

File Explorer has undergone significant improvements, and it now appears to be a lot smoother than it was previously. The Ribbons have been replaced with a modern and streamlined toolbar that contains the most often used commands.

This is a significant improvement over the File Explorer feature in Windows 10, and the redesigned UI is less crowded while still giving you the most important selections. To top things off, there is a new icons collection to choose from.

These are not the sole improvements; the Taskbar and Start Menu have been completely redesigned, and they now have a cleaner, more simplified appearance.

The Taskbar has been centralized, and it resembles that of Chrome OS or macOS. If you don't like the new Start Menu, you could always relocate it to the left -hand side in the Settings application.

Sadly, unlike past editions, the Taskbar is now fixed at the base and cannot be moved to the side or top.

The Start Menu has also been updated, and it now has curved sides like the rest of the windows. Also, you will observe that the Start Menu has been simplified and has lesser apps.

There is now a dedicated applications area that allows users access to their favorite applications swiftly and conveniently. A suggested section appears underneath it, which you may utilize to browse recently accessed files or newly installed programs.

All of your applications are still visible, but they're now buried at the back of the All Apps icon. In comparison to the Windows 10 equivalent, the redesigned Start Menu appears to be much more ordered and basic.

The Notification Center has also been completely redesigned, with a Notifications bar and Quick Settings option replacing the Action Center.

This implies that fast settings are no longer bundled with notifications and may be seen alone. The two fresh panels have curved edges to fit the new Windows 11 style.

Just as importantly, with Windows 11, Microsoft Edge received a redesign that has minimalistic and a basic UI.

We prefer the new Windows 11 appearance, but if you don't like it, you can easily change it to be seen as the Windows 10 interface.

Widgets

Live Tiles have been deprecated in Windows 11 in favor of widgets that provide the same function. Despite their similarities, they do not live on the Start Menu and rather feature their panel.

This appears to be a fantastic addition, and because widgets have got their specific panel, they will not consume as much area as Live Tiles previously did

New Features in Calculator App

The latest update of Windows 11 now brings in new features to the calculator app. More elements and a new design with rounded corners have been introduced.

98

According to Microsoft, the scientific and programmer calculator has now been improved.

In addition, the currency feature in the calculator can now be used to convert up to 100 different currency units.

Calendar and Mail

The calendar app also features few little changes but it still largely remains the same, as it was in Windows 10 except for the new rounded corners and some little icon changes.

There have also been some little changes in the mail app to match with the Windows 11. Although it still looks very much the same as the mail app in Windows 10. One of the noticeable visual changes is the rounded edges of the app.

File Explorer

Windows 11 brings a few changes to file explorer. You'll find that the context menu is now more compact with neatly arranged options to use as little space as it can allow.

At the top left corner of the file explorer is also a *new* option that lets you easily create new files, folders, shortcuts and different documents.

Multitasking Has Been Enhanced

While Windows 10 allows you to snap windows to multiple viewpoints of your monitor to efficiently manage your workplace, Snap configurations take it to a whole new next level.

You may pick from six different layouts to better manage your open apps with this functionality. Snap, on the other hand, will not operate on older displays, so consider that.

Not only that, but with the innovative Snap group function, Windows 11 will remember which programs you previously launched and in what style, allowing you to quickly return to it.

Just mouse over the app in the Taskbar to select the Snap design linked with it and reinstate it, together with all the applications that were previously in it.

Virtual machines are also receiving some upgrades, with the ability to modify the backdrop for every virtual desktop.

Navigating between desktops has also been enhanced, and you can now do so by dragging onto the Task View symbol in the Taskbar and choosing what virtual desktop you'd want.

Changes to dealing with external displays are also included in Windows 11, and windows on an external display will now be remembered once you detach it.

The applications that were running on your system will be reopened immediately once you attach them to this external display, letting you pick up from where you packed up.

This is a nice advance in terms of lifestyle since it should render multitasking on many displays much simpler than previously.

Enhanced Touchscreen Input

The new Windows 11 places a strong emphasis on touchscreen capabilities and offers a novel touchscreen environment. When you're using your gadget in tablet mode, there is no longer a whole-screen Start Menu; rather, icons will feature extra space and be simpler to reach.

There are a few novel touch commands that let you quickly change to the last active program, return to the desktop, or reinstate your active application windows for simpler navigation.

With gestures, you can access Task View and move between virtual desktops and application windows. With a 4-finger flick, you could now move between desktops.

Touch Keyboard now includes additional customization options, and also more themes to pick from, and a novel theme framework that makes it easier to develop fresh theme designs.

Also, the Pen input has been enhanced, and a Pen button has been added to the Taskbar, allowing you to easily start programs that enable pen input.

Haptic feedback is also supported by pens, so you can feel sensations when using them. Finally, voice input functionality is in-built, letting you type words using only your mic.

New Microsoft Edge Features

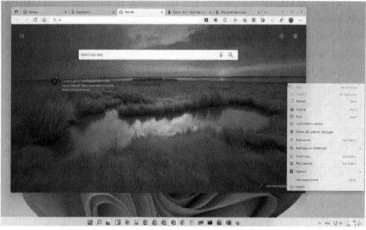

Windows 11 brings in new features to Microsoft Edge 93. You now have new visual changes to the overall browser.

The new Microsoft Edge features semi-transparent menu elements. This means that you can see a little bit of the content at the back of the menu. The Microsoft edge's increased glass-like look now also blends perfectly with the Windows 11 dark theme.

These visual elements may not be enabled by default; therefore, you need to manually turn them on from advanced settings. With the release of the official Windows 11, this feature might be available by default.

To begin, make sure you have the latest version of Microsoft Edge on your Windows 11. If you don't already have this;

- Go to the Microsoft edge insider page and click *download* under the *Canary channel.*
- *Click* Accept and download.
- Once downloaded, launch the new Microsoft edge canary browser.

You can also search for updates for the Microsoft edge if you already have one installed on your PC. To do this;

- Go to *settings* on your browser. Click on the options icon (…) from yourbrowser page and click *settings.*
- Scroll down on the left menu and click *about Microsoft edge.*
- Microsoft Edge will begin a search for an update.

If your Microsoft edge browser is up to date, you can proceed to the next step.

- Open a new tab in the new Microsoft edge canary browser, type in *edge://flag* and press enter. This will open up a Windows experiment page.
- In the search field, type in *Windows 11 visual updates.*
- You'll see an option similar to your search keywords. At the right side of theoption, click the drop down button displaying—default.
- Select enabled.
- Click *restart* at the bottom right corner to apply the changes. This will bringin the new visual changes to your Microsoft edge browser.

Augmented Collaboration

Because Windows 11 is emphasizing on user collaboration, it is no surprise that Microsoft Teams will be included.

As soon as the operating system begins, the program will be accessible from the desktop and available for use. This is akin to what was accomplished with Windows 10 when it came preloaded with Skype.

Because Skype's user base is dwindling and people are migrating to more interactive options, it's no surprise that Microsoft opted to supplant Skyp e with the innovative Microsoft Teams in its Windows 11 offering.

Microsoft Teams appears to be getting some substantial updates shortly, and we anticipate that the incorporation of Microsoft Teams within Windows 11 will be favorably embraced by consumers.

You are not neglected if you are a lover of the Skype application and still utilize it for collaboration with family and friends. There is a method that you can follow to enable the application on your Windows 11-powered device.

Generally, we feel this is a positive step forward, and that the addition of Microsoft Teams will put rival collaboration companies like Slack to the test.

101

Integration with Android Apps

The Intel Bridge feature in Windows 11 allows Android applications to run natively on Windows. Users of AMD-powered should be allowed to operate Android applications directly also, even though this piece of tech may be Intel-based.

Microsoft has partnered with Amazon to provide apps, which implies you ought to be able to install and execute programs from the Amazon App Store if the computer you are using is compliant.

This functionality is brand-new; previously, clients had to utilize Android emulators if they'd like to launch Android applications on their Windows 10-powered PC. This raises yet another pressing question: how will Android emulators work on Windows 11?

From what we've seen thus far, Android emulators would continue to be useful because not every PCs has what it takes to natively run Android applications.

Nevertheless, Google is creating a package known as the Android App Bundles, which is expected to substitute APK files in the future. While this is sure to be very helpful, there may be some compatibility difficulties.

Microsoft Store

Another feature that has been updated in Windows 11 is the Microsoft Store. The redesigned appearance of the Microsoft Store is very obvious that it'll be difficult not to notice it.

The marketplace is now split into double sections: The sidebar and the content pane that allows you to browse certain categories including TV programs, movies, games, and apps.

The revamped marketplace is more minimalistic and slicker than its predecessor. These are not the sole improvements, though.

As aforementioned, the new Windows 11 will execute natively on Android applications, and Android applications can now be downloaded directly from the Store.

The new Store is Win32 programs compliant, which means you'll be able to install and download normal desktop software from it. Progressive Web Apps, Java, React Native, Electron, Xamarin, UWP, and .NET are all supported.

Because the new Microsoft Store can manage browser links, if you decide to download an application through your browser, Store will take charge and download it in the backdrop.

Enhancements to Gameplay

Like we did for others, we must acknowledge the advancements in gaming. Many elements from the newest Xbox Series X have been included in Windows 11 to provide players with the greatest possible gaming experience.

DirectStorage is one of these capabilities, which will enable video games to load quicker from NVMe SSDs. Furthermore, this function will speed up the loading of graphical files, resulting in more realistic game environments.

One functionality worth mentioning is AutoHDR, which allows you to apply HDR upgrades to titles created on DirectX 11 or above.

You can make previous titles more colorful with this functionality, but you'll have to enable Auto HDR in your Windows 11-powered device and have suitable hardware to use it.

The advent of the Xbox Game Pass, which allows you to play the latest release from Bethesda and XboxGame Studios as well as receive access to over one hundred other titles, is arguably the greatest shift with regards to gaming.

Finally, through the Xbox Game Pass Ultimate, you can use a web b rowser to access Xbox Cloud Gaming and play Xbox games on a less -advanced computer.

If you prefer older titles, you will be relieved to learn that you can enjoy them on Windows 11 without encountering tons of problems.

All of these are some great enhancements, and we're excited to witness how Xbox Game Pass and DirectStorage for Windows 11 will perform.

In Windows 11, Microsoft Teams vs. Skype for Business

Video and Audio Calls

Microsoft Teams is a good buddy if you are facing network issues and don't have enough capacity to make a great video or audio conversation. To experience high - quality video or voice with anybody outside or within your company, teams simply need a speed of about 1.2 Mbps.

This programhelps users by allowing themto connect in groups of ten to ten thousand individuals regardless of where they are.

Small businesses with less than twenty workers utilize Skype. Except if you wish to purchase credit to initiate to mobile networks, the software is free.

This business tool lets you host teleconferencing conversations for up to two hundred and fifty people, as well as handle employee identities and give enterprise-grade security.

Chat Functionality

The capabilities of the chat feature are one of the biggest distinctions that exist between the two programs. In this regard, Microsoft Teams does have a significant edge over Skype. Users may be allowed access into any group or private and check its archives whenever they like with Microsoft Teams.

Besides those discussions that were erased singly and for you can do absolutely nothing about, communications remain visible to you irrespective of the time you joined the chat.

The issue with Skype is subtly unique, but it is not to be faulted, although it's one of the best teleconferencing systems available. Chats aren't saved to your history after you have the window closed, but they do allow you the option of adding several connections to a chat group. There's a way to store chat chats, but it requires that you utilize Outlook as your primary email program.

Transferring Files

Microsoft Teams allows you to exchange files even if they're not connected to the internet. You may transmit a wide range of assets, including GIFs, memes, and crucial documentation.

Because Skype doesn't provide an offline solution, you could only exchange files when online. You may, of course, specify file size limitations as well as the kind of items you'd like to transfer.

Guest Access

A guest in Microsoft Teams may start a channel or join a private conversation, exchange an item, and delete, edit, and post messages, which is advantageous over its larger cousin Skype.

Guests who do not yet have a registered Skype account must download the Skype application to attend a session on Skype. The invite is sent to them by calendar or email.

Other Notable Distinctions

When using the new Windows operating system, one of the most noticeable modifications you'll notice is the placement of the Start menu at the screen's center.

This move will have a cosmetic and essential impact, as it'll house commonly used documents and apps, like Microsoft Teams. As a result, the Teams application is incorporated immediately into the Taskbar, allowing you to start talking, sharing files, or phoning with a single click. With a single touch of the Meet icon, you may start calls or add other people.

Also, it is important to note that Meet can be accessed by anybody, irrespective of what computer they're using, or their iOS and Android device, and they do not require a Microsoft account to do so.

Teams are expected to gain popularity as a result of their capacity to transmit text messages on iOS and Android while supporting numerous accounts.

The Meet Now function in Windows 10 will be supplanted by Chat, which will be fully available in your system's taskbar. This new perspective will compel the widespread usage of Skype to be replaced. But Microsoft is not abandoning Skype; it's simply creating a place for its younger sibling Teams.

It's reassuring to know that after switching to Windows 11, you may still install Skype without any costs anytime you wish.

File Explorer in Windows 11

How to Fix Crashing File Explorer

If your file explorer keeps crashing, you'll have to undergo some couple of steps until the problem is fixed.

Step 1: Restart your File explorer

- Your file explorer might need a restart to work properly again. Go to your start menu and search task manager then open the corresponding result to open it. Pressing the *Ctrl + Shift + Esc* on your keyboard.

- Under processes, click *Windows explorer* and tap *restart.*

Step 2: Run using administrative privileges

- You could also fix your file explorer problem by using administrative privileges. To begin, press *Ctrl + Shift + Esc* to open the task manager.

- Inside the task manager, click *file* at the top left corner.

- Click on run new task.

- In the next pop up menu, type in *explorer.*

- Check the box labelled *Check this task with administrative privileges* and click *OK* to apply the changes.

You can also take some measures to prevent your file explorer from crashing in the future. To do this;

- Make sure your file explorer and your task manager are open. Under the processes option in your task manager, right-click file explorer and click *Properties.*

- Under the general tab on the properties page, click *advanced.*

- Make sure to check the options under *file attribute* and uncheck the options under *compress and encrypt* proceed to apply your details.

- Click *OK* to proceed.

- Click *Apply* on the properties page and click *OK* to complete the process.

Step 2: Clear Cache

- Accumulated temporary data has the potential to obstruct the smooth operation of your file explorer. To clear your cache, go to file explorer.

- If file explorer is not in your taskbar, open the start menu and search for fileexplorer then click on the corresponding result to open it.

- Inside file explorer, click on the options icon (…)

- Under the general tab, click *clear* and tap *OK* after the cache has beendeleted.

How to Use Snap Layout in Different Apps

The new snapshot feature lets you snap your apps into different positions and different sizes on your homescreen. The snap layout feature provides the most used layouts and you can use this feature in any app you open on your PC.

Simply open an app and tap the maximize icon at the top right then select a position to place the app. You can fit up to four apps on your screen at once using this snapshot feature. If you close the app while in a snap layout position, windows will remember its last snap layout position the next time you open the app.

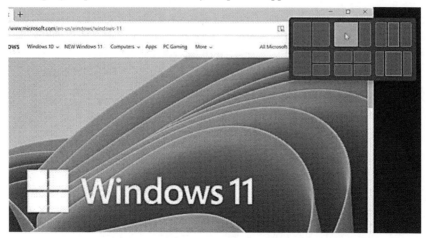

On external monitors, Windows now memorizes the locations of your app layouts so that when you unplug and plug back the monitor, you can still have your layouts arranged just the way it was before you unplugged the cable. In other words, when you unplug the monitor, the layouts do not automatically flood your laptop's screen, rather they are minimized in your laptop's taskbar and then automatically return back to their normal position when you plug the monitor back in.

If you do not like the snap layout feature, you can prevent it from displaying whenever you click on the maximize button. To do this;

- Go to the start menu and click on *settings.*
- Click *system.*
- Tap *Multitasking.*
- Uncheck the option, which says—*show snap layouts when I hover over a window's maximize button.* The next time you click on the maximize icon, you'll no longer get snap layouts.

Settings

The settings feature has seen some changes with the new Windows 11. You now have all settings arranged accordingly. Select a settings folder on the left to see all setting s inside it.

Clipboard paste as text

To do this;

• After copying a text, press **Windows + V.** This will open a clipboard history tab. Click on the options (...) icon and tap **Paste as text.** Your text will now be pasted as plain text.

How to Hide the Windows 11 Taskbar

For those seeking to optimize their workspace and screen size, concealing the taskbar on any Windows platform is a fantastic method to squeeze a bit more out of smaller displays. In all honesty, some people simply want to keep it tucked away. Whichever camp you sit in, here's a short how-to on how to conceal the Windows 11 Taskbar:

• Right-Click The Taskbar

• Then click taskbar settings

Locate The Right Toggle. This will be the **'Automatically hide the taskbar in desktop mode'** option. Activate it by clicking it. The Taskbar will now be hidden.

To display the taskbar, just move the mouse pointer to the base of the screen.

How to Enter BIOS in Windows 11

Having access to your BIOS may be very beneficial. You can monitor the temperature of your CPU, change the fan speeds, and change the sequence in which your computer boots. These menus include almost every detail of the machine's inner workings, so be sure you know what you're searching for before entering! You can even check for a TPM setting in the BIOS to verify whether you're ready for Windows 11!

Advanced Startup

Once identified, you may proceed into Advanced Startup through the **Restart Now option.**

UEFI Firmware Settings

This will take you directly into the BIOS following a restart.

When you wish to leave the BIOS, simply locate the Save & Exit settings to be taken back into the normal Windows boot-up process.

Finding Your IP Address in Windows 11

An IP Address is a one-of-a-kind identification that is automatically given to every device connected to the internet. The Internet Protocol (IP) enables data to be transferred from and to Windows 11 computers. IP addresses vary when linked to various networks and identify your location to offer users location -relevant content, similar to when you move house or vacation. When troubleshooting network problems and setting up routers, knowing an IP address will come in useful.

How can you find your IP address?

Using the Taskbar

Open the Network & Internet Options window.

• To do so, just right-click the network symbol below and choose **'OpenNetwork & Internet Settings.'**

Open Networking and Sharing Center

107

- On the following page, on the left-hand side, click *'Ethernet,'* then *'Network and Sharing Center.'*
- Select the Hyperlink for Connection
- To access the Status Window, click the hyperlink next to the connection field.
- *Go to the* Details tab.
- Lastly, choose *'Details'* from the drop-down menu.

Using the Command Prompt

- Activate the Command Console
- Begin by using the taskbar's search button. Click open after typing in 'CMD.'
- Enter Command
- Once the page has loaded, type *'ipconfig'* on the user line, then press enter. On the 'IPv4 Address line,' the current IP address will be shown.

Through Google *Simply go to Google and type in* "Find my IP address."

The Windows 11 Subsystem for Linux

How to Install Windows Subsystem for Linux (WSL) on Windows 11

WSL is a feature in Windows that allows developers to run Linux GUI programs directly on a Windows device. This feature is an optional one, which means users who need it will have to install it specifically for their use.

To begin the installation process;

- Click on *windows terminal preview* and click *run as administrator*.

- Press *yes* to proceed.

- Type *wsl --install* and press *enter.* Make sure there is a space between Wsl and the dash symbols.

- This will install the tools you need to get WSL running on your system. You might have to wait a little while as the installation continues.

- Once the installation is complete, restart your computer. Go to *start,* click the power button and tap *restart.*

- After signing into your Windows 11, the installation process will continue and you will be required to set up *Ubuntu, which* is a Linux operating system.

- Enter a username and click *Enter* on your keyboard.

- Enter your *password* and click *Enter.*

- Confirm your password and click *Enter* again to complete the installation process.

109

If you want to install a different operating systemfor the linux GUI;

- Go to the **Windows terminal preview** again, click run as administrator, and tap *yes.*

- In the command prompt, Type **wsl --list --online** and press **enter.** Make sureyou leave a space between before the dash symbols.

- When you press enter, you'll get a list of the operating systems you caninstall on your system. This list is categorized by **name** and **friendly**

name.

- To install one of them, type **wsl --install –d** and then type in the name of the operating systemyou wish to download.

- For instance, you can type in **wsl --install -d kali-linux** to install the third option.

- Press **enter** after typing in your Linux OS choice and proceed to enter your username and password to sign you up for your new Linuxoperating system. If you already have the WSL installed on your system, you will not be required to restart your computer when installing a new Linux operating system; however if you're installing a different operating system while also installing the WSL for the first time, you will be required to restart your systembefore you can enter your username and password.

Virtual Machine in Windows 11

A virtual machine is a piece of programming that sudden spikes in demand for your equipment and copies a working framework. VMWare Workstation Player 16, a free (for non-business utilization) virtual machine that is as of now the go-to for Windows 11, will be utilized today. The lone free program can run it effectively.

Directly installing Windows 11 on your primary computer is risky and, in general, ridiculous. You will have to reinstall Windows 10 from the start if the development build of Windows 11 fails in any way and you go over your ten-day restriction before Windows purges the '.old' file from its reserves.

How to Use the Virtual Desktop

Virtual desktops are functionalities where you can launch specific programs on a workspace. Let's say you opened five or six programs, but then, suddenly, you need to meet with a client. Instead of clearing your desktop and preparing it to share your screen, you can come down to the virtual desktop area, click on it, and create a new virtual desktop.

Now at that point, it's going to be a clean start. You can follow up with a c lient, work with them, open new applications, and switch between the multiple virtual desktops in a very easy way by retaining the previous settings. Now for you to go back to the previous desktop, you can hold the mouse on the virtual desktops icon and th en switch to your first virtual desktop, where you'll get access to your Apps and settings and things like that.

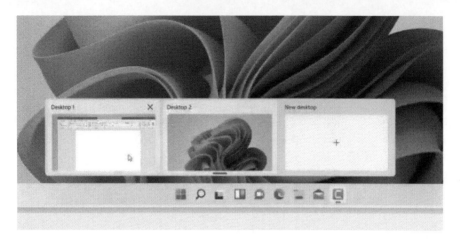

Activate Virtualization in BIOS

Virtualization can now be given a lot more power on modern computers. If the necessary BIOS settings aren't verified first, VMWare Workstation will not boot. This is mostly to protect them from receiving numerous complaints each day about how their program doesn't function; it works, but it requires more than a single CPU core to operate.

For this, we will need to enter the BIOS, which may be done in a few different methods. To get started, restart your computer and press F2, F4, or DEL to enter.

NB: There should be a little notice at the bottom indicating which button will get you in.

Through Windows, you can access the BIOS

Another option is to use Windows. Go to *Settings, Update & Security, and choose Activation* from the sidebar.

Then, under Advanced Start-Up, *select* Restart Now.

Move to Troubleshoot, Advanced Options, and UEFI Firmware Settings on your PC's blue page. Then press the restart button.

Virtualization (Intel and AMD) should be enabled

Now that we have arrived at this stage, you will want to look for an option under CPU Configuration, which is typically found in Advanced Mode.

Intel Systems will need to enable Intel Virtualization Technology, while AMD users would need to enable SVM Mode. The names may vary according to the manufacturer, but this is how it's usually done...

Method 1: VMWare Installation. Grab the file from VMWare's download website and install it.

Method 2: Download the ISO image. This allows you to get a whole ISO from them and install it at a later time.

Method 3: Create a whole new virtual machine. Choose *'Installer disc image file (iso),'* where we want to browse to the ISO that the Windows Media Tool downloaded for us, and then click *'Create a New Virtual Machine,'* which will take you to the Wizard.

Give it a name and a drive large enough to hold your new virtual operating system. I assigned mine to an external SSD to ensure a fast system. You don't want to clog up your C: disk with unnecessary data.

Method 4: Create a Storage Area. Make sure you have enough space to install Windows 11, which is not the recommended size of 60GB. Even though this is for Windows 10, you can set it to 128GB to simulate a laptop of some kind.

Method 5: Modify the system's settings. You should go into the Customize Hardware section before hitting Finish to rejig the specifications you are giving this computer.

Method 6: Add RAM

If your system has 16GB or more, allocate 8GB to yourself; this will enough. For a seamless system, a minimum of 4GB is required.

It will also provide you with two CPU cores, which is more than plenty. Finish by pressing the finish button and restart your computer.

Also, get the VMWare Tools, which will help with emulation.

Install Windows 11 on Your computer

This is the tedious part; just follow the on-screen prompts to enter Windows 11.

Windows Insider's Program

Follow the basic instructions for joining the Windows Insiders Program to get access to the Dev channel and download the latest updates.

Install Windows 11

You'll go through the standard Windows Insider download process, which may take some time, and after it asks you to reboot, Windows 11 will begin to install.

Conclude

Multiple displays, full-screen, and the ability to copy and paste files or screenshots between the two computers are all supported by VMWare. It's the ideal sandbox for anyone who wants to experiment without making any long-term commitments.

When you're through using the virtual computer, just remove it from VMWare or File Explorer and go on with your life as if nothing had occurred.

Installing and Setting up Windows 11 on Raspberry Pi 4

While there has been a lot of talk about TPM 2.0 and the CPU req uirements for Windows 11, leaving users of older PCs concerned about getting their hands on those rounded corners, you can now install Windows 11 on a small, low-powered system called the Raspberry Pi 4.

Because of its cheap nature and time form factor, Raspberry Pis are renowned for toying and people wishing to maybe replicate some old school games, which is why this is such a huge issue. However, now that Pi owners or anyone looking for a pocket - sized PC capable of running an OS of this quality can install and run the exciting new Windows update, it opens up a world of possibilities.

How to Enable Bluetooth Through Settings

With Windows 11's move to a more simplified search engine, all you have to do now is go to the Search Icon (the magnifying glass), select **Settings,** and then **Devices**.

Enable Bluetooth

The toggle switch may be used to turn on Bluetooth from here. If there isn't a toggle, your computer doesn't have a Bluetooth device or it isn't turned on.

A Faster Method Simply press the Search button and enter in **"Bluetooth,"** and you'll be taken right there.

How to Use the Windows Troubleshooter to Repair Bluetooth

Here's how:

Go to Update & Security, then Settings.

Further Troubleshooters On the left, you will see Troubleshoot, which will offer you the choice to use **'Additional Troubleshooters.'** Choose the Bluetooth option and let it run; it should detect any problems with your hardware and either offer a solution or complete the task automatically.

How to Screenshot on Windows 11

Taking a screen capture of your Windows 11 PC screen might be useful when you need to keep a record of the data displayed on your screen or offer what you're seeing on your screen with companions or via web-based media. You can take a screen capture in Windows 11 in an assortment of techniques, contingent upon what you're attempting to do and how you need to accomplish it.

On Windows 11, how do I take a screenshot?

• Snipping Tool. The Snipping apparatus in Windows 11 is a basic and helpful device for catching the full substance of your screen, a specific open Window, or physically picked segregated segments.

You can get the Snipping Tool from the Start Menu or via looking for it, and after you've snapped an image, you can save it or duplicate it to your clipboard.

Despite the fact that the Snipping Tool has been accessible since Windows Vista, it actually works. Notwithstanding, since Microsoft has effectively incorporated a replacement for the Snipping device, it's difficult to foresee when the Snipping Tool will be eliminated in future Windows 11 working framework redesigns.

• Snip & Sketch. This is the Windows 11-viable trade for the Snipping Tool. The two choices get by on Windows 11 for the present, however Microsoft claims that Snip and Sketch will ultimately be the solitary choice.

It has a ton of similar provisions as the Snipping Tool, however it's all the more alluringly stuffed and functions admirably with the Windows 11 warning UI. It's a more refined and all around planned programming that holds similar fundamen tal usefulness as its archetype.

Catching the entire screen, a specific window, or physically catching a particular district all have similar choices. Your image is promptly moved to your clipboard so you might utilize it somewhere else, or you can open it to save it or make explanations.

It tends to be dispatched utilizing the console alternate way "Windows Key + Shift + S," which isn't the least difficult blend of keys to press immediately without some experience. You may likewise utilize the Start menu to begin it.

• *Print Screen* This is a standard Windows highlight that is probably not going to be eliminated very soon. This is such a significant OS highlight that it has its catch on pretty much every Windows console.

Taking a screen capture of whatever is on your screen at the time is just about as straightforward as squeezing

Networking in Windows 11

Computer networks are everywhere these days, and everything seems to be connected to everything else, so it's important to know a little about basic networking to be able to connect your computer to things like other computers, wireless printers, *etc.* After all, the Internet is the world's biggest network, so without networking, we would all be just talking to ourselves… at least when it comes to our electronic gadgets.

Networking with Windows is not all that difficult if you are just setting up a basic home network or small office network. When you start dealing with domains (discussed next) and multiple sites and networks connected together, then thing s get a little more interesting. But if you just want to network a few computers together, then it's fairly easy to do. I'm not going to go through a step-by-step demonstration because there are too many variables that won't relate to your configuration, s o I will just go over the basics.

Workgroups

In order for your computers to be able to communicate with each other on a network, they need to be in the same, let's say "club" if you will. For Windows, this club that your computers are a part of is called a Workgroup. These workgroup computers are all equal when it comes to who is in charge and no computer has any authority over another computer. The default workgroup name for Windows is actually called Workgroup, but you can change it to whatever you like as long as all the computers you want in the workgroup have the same workgroup name as well. All the computers have their own local user accounts, and if you want to access another computer from yours, then you need to have an account on that computer as well.

Domains

If you work at a company with a reasonable number of computers that run Windows, then you are most likely part of a Windows domain. In a domain, all access and security is controlled by centralized servers called domain controllers. You log into your computer with your domain username and password and that determines what level of access you have to all network resources like file servers and printers. Using domains makes it easy for network administrators to control user accounts and permissions since it can all be done from one place and apply to the entire network.

To check your workgroup name or to see if you are a part of a domain you can go to the *System* settings and then the *About* section. Then you will see a link that says Domain or workgroup which you can then click on to take you to screen as seen in figure 10.2. Next to the word Workgroup will be the workgroup name. (In my example it's called WORKGROUP.) If your computer were joined to a domain, it would say *domain* rather than *Workgroup* in this section.

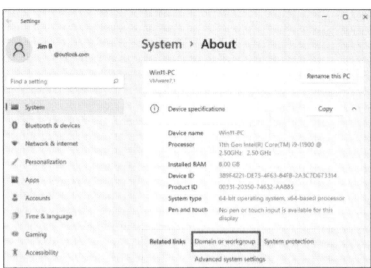

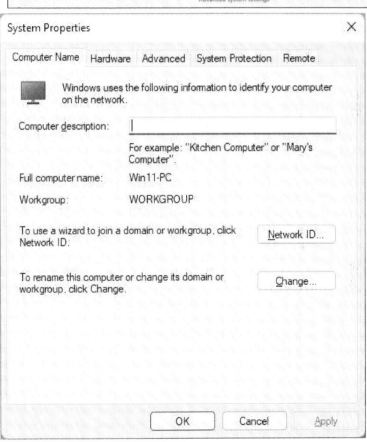

IP Addresses and Configuration

Computers and other devices on a network use IP addresses to communicate with each other. MAC (media access control) addresses are also used for network communication, but that's a story for another day!

An IP address is a number (for the sake of simplicity) that is assigned to a computer that is then used to communicate with other computers and devices that also have an IP address assigned to them. It consists of 4 sets of numbers (called octets) and looks something like this—192.168.10.240. There are several types of address classes, and things can get really complicated, so I will just stick with the basics, so you have an understanding of how IP addresses are used.

When you want to connect to another computer on the network (or even to a website) you can type in its name and then a service called DNS (Domain Name System) translates that computer or website name into the IP address of that computer or web server. That way you don't have to memorize IP addresses and only need to know the computer name or website name. On a network you can't have the same IP address assigned to two devices otherwise there will be a conflict.

There are also what are known as public and private IP addresses. Public IP addresses are used for things such as web servers and are unique to that server (meaning that IP address can't be used on any other public\Internet device in the world). Private IP addresses, on the other hand, can be used by anyone on their internal network a nd assigned to devices that only communicate with other internal devices. That doesn't mean these internal devices can't connect to the Internet or other public devices. To do this, the private IP address is translated to a public IP address through the process of NAT (Network Address Translation). This process is beyond the scope of this book, but feel free to look it up if you want to learn more about it.

So the bottom line is that your computer needs an IP address to communicate on the network and even to get on the Internet. There are a few ways to find the IP address of your computer, and I will now go over what I think is the easiest one. If you open a command prompt (which is a way to run text based commands on your computer as they did before Windows), you can type in a certain command to find your IP address information. To open a command prompt simply type in *cmd* from the search box or from Cortana and you will be shown a window with a black background and flashing cursor.

From this box, all you need to do is type in the command *ipconfig* to be shown the basic IP configuration of your computer (figure 10.4). Keep in mind that the information given here will vary from computer to computer based on how many network connections you have, such as wireless and Ethernet (plugged in), and so on.

For now, you only need to be concerned with the IPv4 address, but soon we will all be using IPv6 addresses since we are out of publicly available IPv4 addresses to assign to new public devices. You might also notice that I have a network connection for a Wireless LAN adapter but it's not in use so therefore it doesn't have an IP address. You need to know which network interface you are dealing with when running this command to get the information you need.

Dynamic and Static IP Addresses

One more thing I want to mention about IP addresses is the difference between a static IP address and a dynamic IP address. Each one has its place in networking, so it's important to know the basic difference between the two.

119

DHCP

I want to mention DHCP really quickly since I was just talking about it in the last paragraph. DHCP (Dynamic Host Configuration Protocol) simplifies the management of IP address configuration by automating address configuration for network clients. In order for DHCP to work, you need to have a device acting as a DCHP server. This device can be a computer, router, or another type of network device.

How to Connect to a Wi-Fi Network in Windows 11

Your wireless router transmits data via radio waves to all connected devices like your TV, smartphone, tablet, and computer. Since they communicate over airwaves, your devices and personal information become vulnerable to hackers, cyber-attacks, and other threats.

You may experience this, especially when connecting to public Wi-Fi networks at places such as a coffee shop or an airport. In the event of a wireless network that isn't password-protected, you should take advantage of a personal hotspot. Almost all smartphones have a personal hotspot feature which means you can access the internet on your laptop by connecting it to your phone.

There are various brands providing wifi services at an affordable rate. All you need to do is select the best one for you. You might want to consider price and internet speed when choosing.

In this section, we will demonstrate how to connect to the internet from a Windows PC. So if you have a Windows PC with a network wired connection, take the wired connection and plug it into the provided port on your PC, and you should be able t o connect to the internet. If you have a wireless laptop or a wireless device with Windows 11 and you want to connect to a network, whether at home or your business, you'll see a globe with a little arrow in the bottom right on your screen. Click in that area. It doesn't matter which area, and it will bring up quick settings.

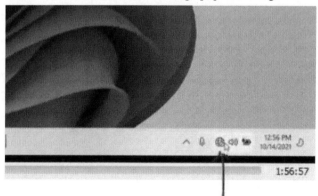

Notice that currently, the wi-fi is not turned on, so you can click to turn it on, then it now turns to blue. So typically, that has to be blue. It has changed during Windows 11.

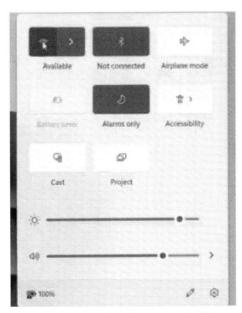

So once it is blue for the wireless connection, that means that it's on and available to view the wireless networks. Then you need to click on the right arrow shown in the image below for the wireless connections.

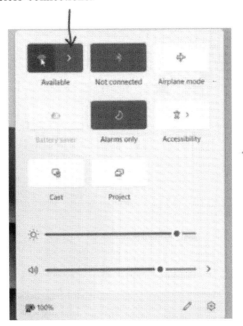

Pick the connection in your area or fromyour business, typically the ones that have a lock. That needs a passphrase, and you need to know the passphrase on your router. Print it out from the internet provider or in a business, and it might be a shared password through a department or, in many cases, upon login. Click on the network connection, and then click connect. It will prompt you to enter the passwords.

The little icon can check additional properties related to the wireless Network.

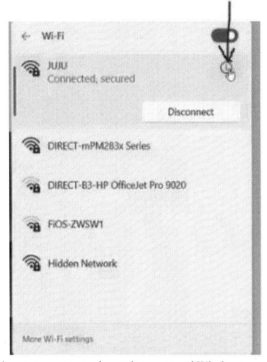

To get to these settings, you can go to the settings area and Windows search. Then choose wi-fi settings and then select show wireless networks. That is where you pickto connect to a network. So that's another way to manage the Wireless Network and connect to a Network.

How to Connect to the Internet

It is very basic, but it's one of the aspects of learning about an operating system, particularly if you're not sure how this is done. Once you have connected your computer to the Network, you need to use a wired or wireless browser. Now the default browser is included in Windows 11, which is the Microsoft edge.

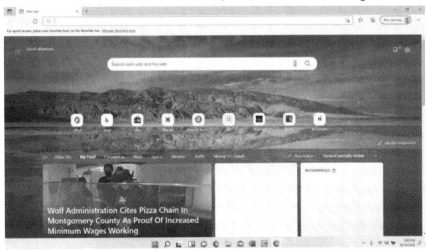

The Microsoft Edge is typically based on a chrome background platform, but it's very efficient. Now, of course, other browsers are also good, like google chrome, firefox, and other ones such as brave, which is a recent one based on chrome. But for more privacy, notice that you have a search box on the bottom and an address bar on the top where you type your URL.

It can also search, so you'll get many other things if you type in on the Search . It'll perform a search because the address bar on the top acts as both a navigation tool and a search tool. They are combined into one.

Now a lot of users search in the search box.

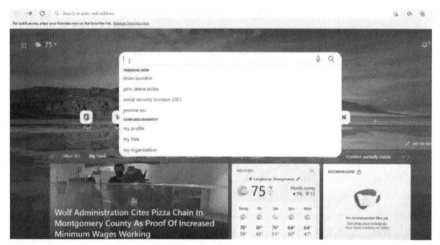

So, for example, whenever you type in casselli.com, that will not take you directly to the website you're searching as part of the startup page's default search. So it's going to give you a lot of different options but not necessarily take you directly into the site. So my suggestion is that to be effective and know how this is done, you type in what you want on the top part and not the second part.

The other thing to consider for the web browsers is to check the settings. To modify the settings in your browser, click the icons on the top right and go to settings.

Then on your settings, you can change the privacy or appearance look and feel of your browser. The starting page is where you can set a new page. For example, if you want to always start with a new page and the new page is conseli.com, that's where you add it in.

Changing the default start page will take you to the website you configured earlier once you open it up again. One of the tools you will find useful is on the three dots up by the right on the settings. Then under more tools, there is an option to cast t his device to connect to a remote display.

Setting up a VPN

What the user needs to set up a VPN is VPN-aware routers and firewalls to allow legitimate VPN traffic to pass unhindered. VPN appliance, concentrator or server to handle and manage incoming VPN traffic and to establish and manage VPN sessions and their access to network resources.

VPN helps to keep your identity secure on the internet and prevents you from being tracked. You can simply download a VPN app to create a VPN for you; however, you can also set up your VPN manually. To begin;

- Right-click on the *network* icon at the bottom right corner of your desktop and select *open network and internet settings*.
- *Click* network and sharing.
- *Click on* setup a new connection or network.
- *Click* Connect to a workplace *and tap* next.
- *Click* use my internet connection (VPN).
- Type in the internet address of your administrator and enter a destinationname of your choice.
- Click *Create.*
- After the creation, click *Change adapter settings* to make some adjustment to yournew VPN.
- Right-click the VPN and select *Properties.*

- Under the properties page, click on *security.* If you know the specific VPN you are connecting to, select it under the VPN type. If not, you can leave the type as automatic. If you have specific information about the VPN, you can adjust these settings according to that information to help you connect faster to the network. In most cases, information about VPN can be found on the network provider's website.

Another way to create VPN in Windows 11 is through the settings page.

- Open the start menu and select *settings.*

- Click on *network and internet* on the left menu.

- Tap VPN.

- Click Add VPN.

- Select *Windows (built-in)* as the default VPN Provider.

- Enter the *connection name* of your VPN. This could be a name of your choice.

- Enter the *server name or address* of the VPN network provider.

- Under *VPN type,* you can select a specific type for your VPN if you have the information but if you do not know the type of VPN you're connecting to, just select automatic and proceed.

- Under *type of sign-in info,* enter the username and password of the network if it is a paid network. If the VPN is free, you can skip this option.

- Click *Save.* You can now connect to your VPN. For quick VPN connection, click on the quick settings panel in the taskbar and tap VPN.

Android Applications in Windows 11

An application is a software program that allows you to perform specific tasks. You find applications in most of your devices like your smartphones, computer, and tablets. Some apps help you to complete certain tasks while others are just for fun. Apps that run on your desktop or laptop computers are known as Desktop applications while those apps that run on your smartphones, tablets are known as Mobile Applications. Some of the apps that work on your mobile devices can also work on your computer and vice versa.

Examples of Desktop applications are *Microsoft Office, Web Browsers, Windows Media Player, Games,* etc. Examples of Mobile Applications are *WhatsApp, Instagram, Gmail, Facebook,* etc. Apps are about communication, productivity, entertainment, and more. With so many possibilities you are sure to find several apps that are perfect for the things you do.

How to Install Android Applications on Windows 11

Android apps are those applications that run on your smartphone or tablet. The new Windows 11 operating systemnow allows you to install and run android apps on your system. You will need to install the subsystem for android and also the Amazon store to be able to run them.

To be able to install android apps on your Windows 11, you must first check if your system meets up with the requirements to install them. Below are the requirements you need before you can install android applications;

The OS build of your system must be *22000* or more.

The installed RAM should be at least *8 gigabytes*.

You need to be in the *Beta Channel* of the Windows Insider Program.

You will enable *virtualization* for your PC. To enable virtualization on your pc, simply click on the *Search icon* on the taskbar and search for *Turn on or off Windows features*. Click on it. On the menu, enable the *Virtual Machine Platform* option and that of the *hypervisor* option.

You will need to have the latest version of the *Microsoft store*. Go to the settings of the Microsoft store and check for updates. Make sure you have the latest updates.

The only disappointing thing here is that this only works if your region is set to the *United States*. If you are not in the US region, then you will likely need a *VPN* for it to work. But you can set your region on your system. Simply go to the settings of your computer, search for *region*. Then, on the *country or region* option, make sure that it is set to the United States. This should work but if it doesn't, then you need to use a VPN.

You need to have a *US-based Amazon account* to use the Amazon Appstore. You can also create that using a VPN.

Once your computer meets up with the requirements, you can now proceed to download and install Windows Subsystem for Android. Simply follow the steps below;

Open the *Microsoft Store*. On the search box, search for *Amazon Appstore*.

Click on it and click *Install.* Then, click *Set Up.*

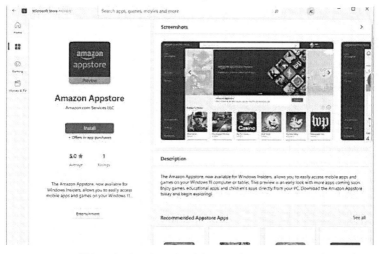

On the prompt, you will be asked to download the *Windows Subsystem for Android*. Click on *Download*.

The download process will take a while. Once the download is done, click *Next*, then *Restart your computer*. After your system has restarted, the Amazon Appstore and the Windows Subsystem for Android should be installed on your PC.

Now, you will need to set up your Amazon Appstore. You will need to *sign in* with your Amazon account. Once you are done signing in, the Appstore is now ready for you to browse and install Android apps.

To install an Android app, simply,

Go to the Amazon Appstore.

Search for the App you want to download. Click on the *GET* option to install it on your system.

The app will be downloaded and will work like other desktop apps on your computer.

You can pin your Android apps to the taskbar or on the Start menu.

Android Windows Subsystem

Applications can be found on the Amazon Appstore. an SSD, 8GB RAM, and a compatible engine (Qualcomm® SnapdragonTM 8c, AMD RyzenTM 3000, Intel® CoreTM i3 8th Generation, or higher) are all required. As the technology is pushed out to certain locations, further information regarding appropriate system requirements would be published.

5G Compatibility: Where accessible, 5G compatibility necessitates the use of a 5G enabled modem.

Auto HDR needs an HDR display.

BitLocker to Go: A USB flash drive is required (accessible in Windows Pro and higher versions).

Client Hyper-V: Needs a chipset with SLAT competencies (accessible in Windows Pro and higher versions).

Cortana: Needs a speaker and microphone and is presently accessible in Canada, Brazil, Australia, Germany, France, China, Japan, Italy, India, Mexico, the United States, the United Kingdom, and Spain on Windows 11.

DirectStorage: To run and store video games that utilize the DirectX12 GPU and Standard NVM Express Controller driver with Shader Model 6.0 compatibility, you'll need an NVMe SSD and a DirectX12 GPU with Shader Model 6.0 support.

DirectX 12 Ultimate: accessible with compatible graphics and games hardware.

Presence: necessitates the use of a detector that can sense human proximity to the gadget or desire to engage with it.

Smart Teleconferencing: A microphone and speaker, microphone, and video camera are required for smart teleconferencing.

Multiple Voice Assistant: A speaker and microphone are required.

Snap 3-Column Layouts: a screen with a width of 1920 active pixels or more is required.

Unmute/mute from the Taskbar: a video camera, microphone, and speaker are required. To activate global, unmute/mute, the application must be compliant with the capability.

Spatial Sound: needs supporting software and hardware.

Microsoft Teams necessitates the use of a speaker, a microphone, and a video camera.

Touch: This feature needs a multi-touch monitor or screen.

2FA Authentication: necessitates the use of biometric (lit IR camera or fingerprint scanner), PIN, or a phone with Bluetooth or Wi-Fi capabilities.

Voice Typing: needs a computer with a mic.

Wake on Voice necessitates the use of a Modern Standby power model as well as a microphone.

Wi-Fi 6E: new drivers and WLAN IHV hardware, as well as a Wi-Fi 6E compliant router/AP, are required.

Windows Hello needs a camera designed for fingerprint scanner or near IR imaging for biometric identification. Windows Hello may be used using a PIN or a compact Microsoft-approved private key on devices that don't have biometric detectors.

Windows Projection: A screen adapter that facilitates Windows Display Driver Model 2.0 and a Wi-Fi device that facilitates Wi-Fi Direct is required for Windows Projection.

Xbox application: An Xbox Live account is required to use the Xbox application, which isn't accessible in every country of the globe. For the most updated availability detail, you want to visit Xbox Live Countries and Regions. A valid Xbox Game Pass membership is required for several functionalities in the Xbox application (marketed individually).

When upgrading to Windows 11, here's a list of all the key features that will be deprecated or removed.

(CPU) Central Processing Unit in Windows 11

The CPU which stands for Central Processing Unit is the most important part of a computer. It is known as the brain of the computer. It provides processing power to the computer. Everything you do on your computer goes through the CPU which makes it an essential part of every PC. The CPU performs millions of tasks and calculations within a second. All the arithmetic calculations and logical operations take place in the CPU.

The CPU has two parts; The Control Unit and The Arithmetic Logic Unit. The Arithmetic unit is the mathematical brain of the computer. They are responsible for performing addition, subtraction, multiplication, division as well as logical operations on the computer. It does all the computation on the computer. The Control Unit controls all the hardware operations on any computer-like input, output, storage, and processing. It reads and interprets instructions and determines the sequence for processing data.

How to Boost Your Processor or Cpu Speed on Windows 11

The new Windows 11 operating system is known to be very much impressive and faster compared to the other versions. The new features of the operating system, make it offer a unique digital experience. Even with all these features, your processor may be running slow while performing some tasks on your computer. This may be caused by low RAM, too many startup programs running on your operating system, low disk space, malware, and viruses, etc.

So, how can you boost your processor or CPU speed on Windows 11?

There are many ways you can make your windows 11 work faster. We are going to show you the different ways you can do this.

Adjust the Performance Power Plan Settings.

Click on the *Search icon* on your taskbar and search for *Control Panel*. Click on it.

133

Click on the drop-down arrow beside the *view by* option and select *Large files*. Then, click on *Power options*.

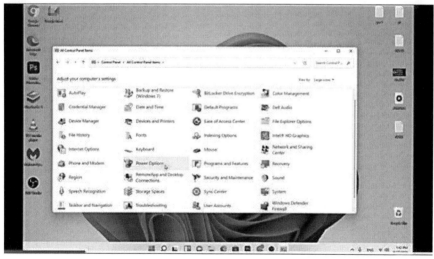

On the High-performance option, click on *Change plan settings*.

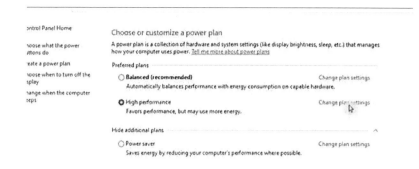

Click on *Change advanced power settings*. On the Advanced settings menu, scroll down and select *Processor power management*.

On the Minimum processor state, change the settings from *50% to 100%*.

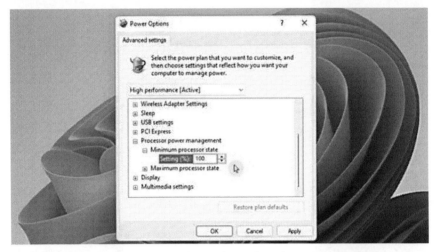

On the maximum processor state, change the settings from *50% to 100%*.

Then, click *Apply* and *Ok*. Refresh your Computer.

How to Factory Reset on Windows 11

Factory reset cleans and reboots the entire system of the computer. It makes the computer function again in a new form. If you don't back up your files before performing the factory reset, you will lose the files. A factory reset clears everything on your computer except the software which will be restored to its default state.

To factory reset on Windows 11, just

Click on the *Windows Start button* and select *Settings*.

Click on *Update and Security*. Then, click on *Recovery*.

136

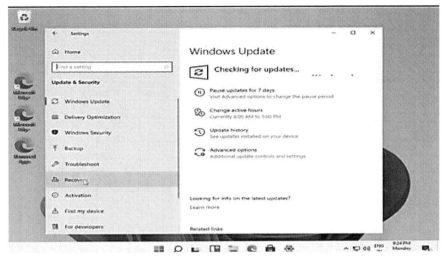

On the right-hand side of the Recovery menu, click on *Reset this PC*.

On the next menu, you will be given two options; if you would want to keep your files or remove everything.

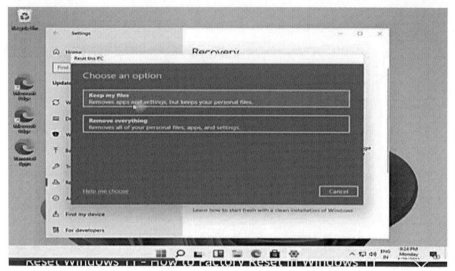

Reset Windows 11 - How to Factory Reset in Windows 11

If you click on the keep your files option, you will be asked how you want to reinstall your Windows operating system. If you want to download it using *Local reinstall* or from *Cloud*.

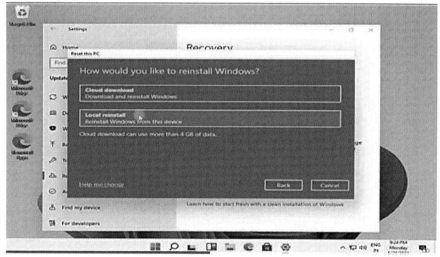

If you select the Cloud option, it will download Windows (from Cloud Servers) and install it on your computer and this will take a lot of time depending on your internet connection. If you select the Local reinstall option, it will reinstall Windows using the already installed Windows.

Once you are done reading the outcomes, click on the *Reset button* to begin the process. This will take some time to finish resetting the Windows and do not interrupt the power connected to the PC. If in the process, you have a power failure, th e installation process will corrupt and the current operating system may not be accessible and because of that, you will have to install Windows from the beginning.

When the resetting is complete, it will direct you to the login interface. When you log in, it begins to customize your Windows settings just like the settings you make when you install Windows for the first time.

Windows 11 Security Setting

The main security feature of Windows Security Essentials was always intended to be a completely optional system that would be installed when people specified which kinds of programs they wanted to be allowed to run. It wasn't a fully -featured antivirus tool, but it was supposed to do some basic stuff, including an ability to detect and remove malware, and offer protection against malware delivered in email or other messages. It was particularly useful for people who had limited knowledge about computer security or who didn't have time to install Windows Defender because they had to be writing code or performing other critical tasks.

In Windows 11, Windows Defender is being replaced by Microsoft Security Essentials—as it was originally called—along with Windows Defender Antivirus. These are the same features as in Windows 10 but they're now being integrated into a single system that's more easily managed and is meant to be an "integrated solution."

There are a few easy steps to set up Windows 11 and mobile devices to lock down your security settings, but first, you need to access your settings. The Microsoft Account section can be accessed by clicking on My Microsoft Account and then clicking Settings & Privacy.

From there, go to Accounts & Privacy and click the Security category. From there you will see a list of features and sections.

The options are fairly self-explanatory. At the bottom of the Security section, select the page with your privacy options to show your Settings.

This page gives you options for resetting passwords, setting up two -step verification, adding a trusted device, and more. All of thes e options are disabled by default but can be enabled by making sure you disable "Settings without an account" and choose "Manage" under Trust Centre.

How to Customize Privacy Setting

Let's look into how to customize the privacy settings in Windows 11. Go to the Start menu, on the search bar, type privacy settings. Notice on the left, you'll have privacy and security.

Then you can change other things related to security as well. But in this case, you are concerned primarily about the privacy settings. In general, in your privacy & security, you might want to turn off many options. The same applies to speech settings under privacy. You can go to the speech settings and turn it off.

Suppose you're not sending a speech pattern to be stored externally from yo ur PC. Then go to the inking and type in personalization, and turn that off. You can turn off the dictionary, certain terms, and words that you type on the soft keyboard. Additionally, go to the diagnostic and feedback. You need to potentially turn off all of them. Then on the feedback frequency, input the most minimum frequency that it allows you to put in. But of course, take note of what you're turning off just in case something happens you'd come back to them.

If you go to the activity history, you can choose to turn it off as well. You can clear the privacy setting and then go to the search permissions for the safety of kids or the moderate Search that has to do with the web content. It's going to be displayed on your computer.

On your location, notice that there are also app permissions such as location. That is very similar to a smartphone or an iPhone, where you can control what apps can access your GPS location. That is the same thing as well. You're just going to identify which apps will have access to your location settings, and you can change that by default or clear the history. The same is with the camera and microphone.

However, for the camera and microphone, you'll be cautious of turning things off. For example, if you're turning things like skype off, you're not allowing the camera to turn on when using skype. For some specific Apps, when you go to use them, the app will most likely have problems with using the camera or the microphone. So you would be very cautious about turning off the camera settings. Voice activation can be kept off, and the Cortana too.

How to Use Quick Setting Center

This section will go through how to use the action center or quick settings center in Windows 11. Typically in the taskbar on the far right of the des ktop, you have a listing of items or functions that you can quickly access.

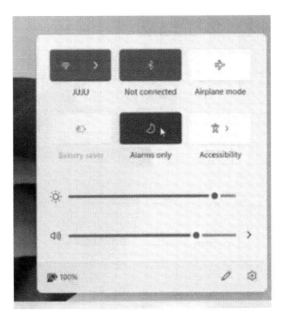

Any icon in blue indicates active, while those that are not in blue are not activated. At this point, you can change the display, sound settings, volume settings, *etc*. Now notice that there is also an edit icon on the bottom. When you click on the edit, you can add additional items to the quick settings area, but I wish Microsoft would have added these additional settings by default. So if you click on + (add), let's say you want a cast option to connect to a remote display easily, or you want a night light option, nearby sharing, or even a project option. So when you select any of your choices, then click on done. Now those options will be available at any point by simply clicking anywhere on your eye view icon and then selecting that particular option for quick access.

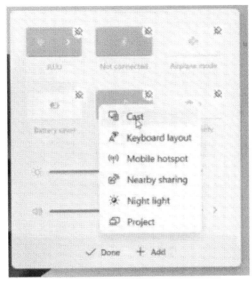

How to Change a Default Printer

This section will demonstrate how to change the default printer or set up the default printer in Windows 11. By default, in Windows 11, Windows determines which printer becomes the default. So to set the default printer, Go to the search menu and type in printers.

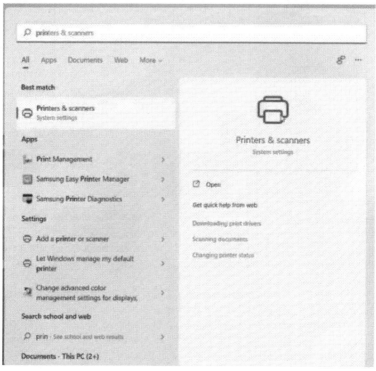

Go to printers and scanners, and then the first option you would turn off on the list of printers is, let "Windows manage my default printer." Once you have turned off the option for Windows to manage the printer, go to the particular printer you want. Then click on it, then a set as default button will show up on the top right to make it your default.

How to Connect to Windows 11 Store

Think of the Windows 11 store as the app store on your iPhone or Google store for Android smartphones. To access the App store, click on the Windows start menu or the Search. Then you can search the store or click on the Microsoft store.

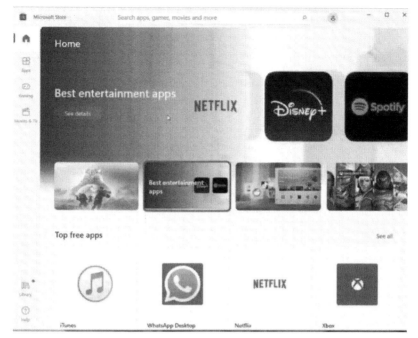

These are third-party apps that you can add to your PC to increase its functionality. There is also in Windows 11 functionality an option to install Android Apps, and you do that primarily through the Amazon App store. So if you want an app installed, whether Netflix, WhatsApp, or whatever is the app, click on the app, and then sometimes you might have to pay an additional fee or may not. You can check the rating, description, and so on. If you decide to install, click on the app, then click on Get.

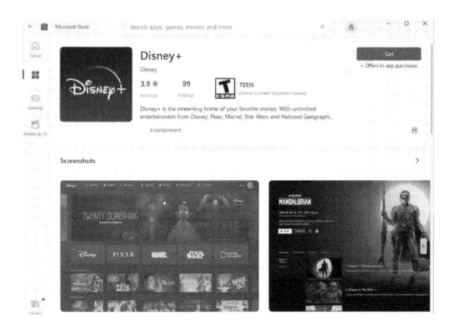

145

It will associate the app with your Microsoft account. You'll need to enter your Microsoft account login, and it's very similar to an App Store from Apple or Google on smartphones.

How to Change Your Windows Password

In this section, you are going to learn how to change your Windows password. There are a couple of ways to change it. If you're working in a corporate environment or connected to a network, you will change the password through the IT department's tools. However, in most cases, like a network account, you can change your Windows password by simply pressing Ctrl Alt Delete on your computer, and then a prompt like an image below will come up.

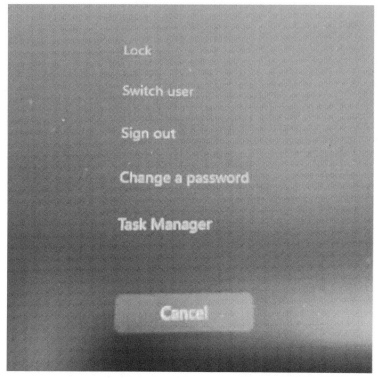

Then you can click on change password, put in your old password followed by the new password and confirm the new password. That is the quickest and easiest way to change the password.

The other options are also on the Search. If you go to Search, you have more clicks involved in the procedure on the change password, but you'd still reach the same conclusion.

How to Lock Your Computer

We will demonstrate how to lock your computer. If you're going to step away from your desk for a few minutes or the rest of the day, this is a very good practice to get into the custom of locking your device. It is for security and maintaining your privacy and the security of your files. So on any application you are working on or at any point you want to lock your computer, press the Windows key and the letter L on the keyboard.

Then it will bring you back basically to the login screen again. When you're ready to come back and start working again, hit any keys on the keyboard, enter your password, and then you're back to everything that you had on your computer. If you want to do it using the Windows option, go to the Windows s tart menu. The option is located on the start menu. Click on your account at the bottom left of the start menu. You will see an option for a lock on your account.

Window Security Settings

In this segment of Windows 11, you will go over the Windows security settings and check your computer for viruses and malware. Windows 11 come packaged with its security suite and firewall tools as well. One of the ways to get to the tools is to open the start menu and search for Windows security on the search window.

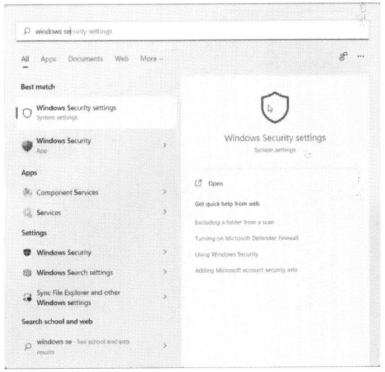

147

Go to windows security settings, and it will give you a preview of actions necessary for your computer, like things that are ok on your computer and so on. Now to customize those settings, click open Windows security, and then you can set up one drive if you prefer to. It is not a necessity, and it is Microsoft pushing one drive and trying to make sure that you're backing up your files online on the cloud and not necessarily losing them at some point in time.

Then under the account, protect login with the Microsoft account. On the left-hand side, you have the firewall and network protection. Note, there are no actions needed at this point, but you can click on it and check various firewall rules, advanced settings and customize the firewall settings if you wish.

You can block unwanted apps on the App and browser control and make sure it's turned on. Put in your password, and it will enable it for you. There are additional settings behind the scenes that it's utilizing on the device security, such as the s ingle-core isolation, security processor level, *etc.*

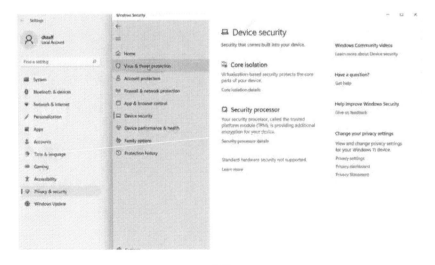

If you go on virus and threat protection on the left-hand side, this is where you can run a scan on your computer. You can do a quick scan that can take minutes depending on the device or change the scan options and do a full scan or a custom scan. Once you pick the type of scan you want, click on scan now. It may take quite a bit of time if you have a lot of files when you select the full scan option.

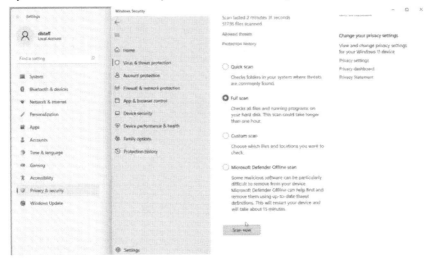

The scanned files will show you the results and things you need to correct or allow. You need to proceed with a positive way to remove them or apply what Microsoft determines. You can also check for a protection history and what has taken place at certain points in time. It's a log of the activity from the scanning software.

So on the security center, you have a virus, firewall protection, account protection, firewall, network protection aspect, browser level protection, device security at the component level in the computer, and device health.

In your Windows security, it's important to note that there is also a family option. You can set it up to protect the kid's screen time habits. So you can set time for kids like how long they can use the devices and so on.

149

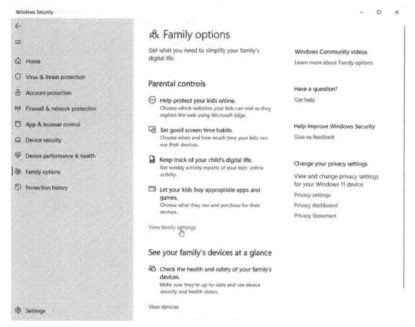

To do that, go to view family settings and configure it using your Microsoft account. All the devices connect to a Microsoft account, and Microsoft manages the time and settings that you have configured for your family.

Using a Password Manager

In terms of managing your passwords, you can use either the built-in password manager app or a third-party one. There are a few password managers you can use: 1Password, Dashlane, LastPass, Keeper, and RoboForm, but we recommend using an account manager.

How to Create a New Secure Password

After clicking Keychain, you will be taken to the page with the password creator. Microsoft recommends creating a password with a minimum of 14 characters. The longer the password, the longer it will take to crack it.

It's also a good idea to write down this password as well. Remember, you want to make it as difficult as possible to crack a password, so the more ways you have to create it, the more the hacker has to go through to break it.

You can get pretty creative with your passwords. But, be sure to use uppercase letters, symbols, numbers, and special characters.

Locate the section on your Microsoft Account home page with your security options, and click this link for Advanced Security. From there you can change your password rules for the account and make it even harder to crack your new passwords.

How to Change Password Rules for Microsoft Account

Find your selected Microsoft Account from the dropdown menu on the page and click the password menu to reveal the Changing Password section. Click the Change Password button.

Disable risky cloud features

Cloud services are great when it comes to keeping your files and contacts organized, but they also make it easier for hackers to access your files.

Windows 11 includes apps like OneDrive, which you can use to store documents and media files.

While you can create multiple OneDrive accounts, we recommend limiting what you share to only the account you are actively using.

How to Disable OneDrive

Head to Settings on your Microsoft Account page, then click on the cloud settings category. Click on the Manage privacy option under cloud services and click on the button for your OneDrive account. Click the Remove button to remove your OneDrive account.

Open Settings on your Microsoft Account page, click on the cloud settings category, then click on the OneDrive item. Click the button Remove OneDrive to remove your OneDrive account.

Set Up a Second Email Address for Your Microsoft Account

When you want to set up a new email address for your Microsoft Account, go to the Trust Centre, click on a category and then choose the Set up a new email account. Then enter your login details for your new email account, and click Next.

This will allow you to configure your account to be used for Microsoft products like Outlook, Windows, Skype, and Xbox Live.

Once your Microsoft Account is set up to use an email address from your Microsoft account, you can set it up to use your new email address as a replacement for the one you use for your Microsoft Account.

Go to the Trust Centre in your Microsoft Account page, and click the Trust you want to set up the account with.

The new account will be called email@yournewaccount.com, while the other email account you use for your Microsoft Account will be called email@youraccount.com.

Decide What Services You Share with Microsoft

While using a password manager such as Dashlane, you should also consider how you're going to share your account information with other people.

The easiest way to share your Microsoft Account with others is to use your own Microsoft account. This way they can log into your Microsoft account from any computer or device with a browser.

Dashlane includes this option in its software, so when you log in to your Microsoft Account, the password manager automatically signs you in. However, it does mean that everyone in your family has access to your account information and passwords.

How to Set a Microsoft Account Password

While you can set up a password manager such as Dashlane, you should also consider how you're going to share your account information with other people.

The easiest tore your Microsoft Account with others is to use your own Microsoft account. This way they can log into your Microsoft account from any computer or device with a browser.

Dashlane includes this option in its software, so when you log in to your Microsoft Account, the password manager automatically signs you in. However, it does mean that everyone in your family has access to your account information and passwords.

Windows Defender Security Center

Previously known as Security Essentials, Windows Defender has been the feature of Windows since the dawn of the PC era and is intended to provide basic malware protection from a variety of threats. It isn't regularly updated by Microsoft, though: whenever malware gets better at evading detection by changing the way it tries to evade detection, Windows Defender tries to adjust its defenses in order to counter the threats. Microsoft's system for estimating the impact of new threats is called Behavior Shielding, and in Windows system is described as a "known-good" filter, similar to those on PCs today. In Windows 11, however, Microsoft is talking about Behavior Shielding as an "exploit mitigation technique" to "completely eradicate known exploits and exploits that are being developed today." To be clear, it's impossible to say if and when Microsoft will change its definition of "known" to mean "better at finding and blocking new exploits," or if the system is as "exploit -mitigation" as Microsoft claims.

Admins and other high-level users who manage multiple PCs or devices have long been able to use Defender to manage which programs are allowed to run. For example, if a program called Spyware Removal Tool was installed in the current system (it doesn't seem to be installed by default), Windows Defender would block it unless it was a trusted program. The changes in Windows 11 will add a new layer to that approach. On the old system, Windows Defender "decides" whether a program can run. If it determines that a program is not allowed to run because it's a malicious program, it will either disable that program or just block it from being run at all. The new system will allow administrators to define what types of programs and what programs, to what extent, will be allowed to run, and how the system will monitor for suspicious behavior and prevent those behaviors.

Other changes in Windows 11 will also increase the visibility of which apps are running on the system. Windows Defender will be able to let you know when an app is writing to disk, and in some cases, it will even let you know when an app is doing something malicious. If you don't want an app to write to disk and thereby leave "fingerprints" that can be used to infer other behavior, the app won't be allowed to write to disk at all.

Although it's getting phased out in Windows 11, Windows Defender does still offer some benefits if you use Windows Defender Antivirus or Windows Defender Security Center. The first is that it offers an overview of your security settings. If you launch Windows Defender Security Center, you'll find the Security Center ribbon on the left side of the screen. By default, this will display Windows Defender Antivirus and Windows Defender Security Center buttons. These are limited to the categories that you're signed into on the appropriate installation of Windows Defender Antivirus or Windows Defender Security Center. If you don't want the same options shown in this overview, you can create your own categories to restrict them. This is great if you've installed antivirus protection from more than one vendor, and you don't want them displayed here.

To configure the categories, click the Change the display of categories button and then click Manage categories. You can add new categories, modify the existing categories, and clear the existing categories. The Security Center also lets you toggle on or off features that can be used to diagnose and fix problems with your system, such as Windows Repair Center or Windows Information Protection.

You can launch a full system scan right from the window. However, you'll only get the results when you're signed in with your Microsoft account. If you're not signed in, you'll be prompted to sign in to enable a full scan.

Windows Defender Security Center also provides some backup options. If you're experiencing a problem with Windows Defender Antivirus, or you're upgrading to Windows 11, or you're accidentally removing the product from your system, you can create a recovery image. To get there, sign in to Windows Defender Security Center, click Manage options, click Reinstall from system recovery, and then click Create a new recovery image. This creates an image of your system that Windows Defender Antivirus can restore should you need to reinstall it. The systemimage is stored in the Windows Components folder under C: Windows Components \Installer and is formatted to look like a Microsoft CD.

Windows Defender Antivirus and Windows Defender Security Center can't do as much as some of the best antivirus programs. For example, you can 't create custom-protected drive folders. You can, however, have both Windows Defender Antivirus and Windows Defender Security Center run automatically at startup. Both products automatically scan your system at sign-on and provide a status report if an infection is found. Furthermore, when you open and select an icon in your Windows tray, it's either Defender Antivirus or Security Center. With each, you'll see basic protection settings such as whether to scan and clean up temporary files, view the current firewall status, and more.

Windows Defender Internet Security is essentially an interface to Windows Defender Antivirus. If you've run into problems with Windows Defender Antivirus in the past, you can use this application as a kind of troubleshooting service. The interface looks somewhat like the Windows Defender Antivirus scan results window, though in this case, you get the results, you don't have to do anything to take advantage of them.

When you open Windows Defender Internet Security, the Productivity tab is active. Click its icon, and the Tab Properties option appears. There you can open the Antivirus Compatibility Viewer, a report that gives you details on which browser and apps support your security software. You also get links to Internet Explorer antivirus and Windows Defender Security Center settings. If you haven't installed the security software, Windows Defender Security Center's options panel offers access to app troubleshooting, such as your security status and the app list, if any. I think it's good that you can always see which antivirus apps have turned up after you've installed Windows Defender Internet Security.

Troubleshooting might be useful, but the Windows Defender site also has an excellent free product support option. You answer a s eries of questions, such as whether you're having trouble installing, and if that's the case, you're immediately connected to a live, human operator. In my experience, most customers don't need this level of service, and so I don't rate the chance that the experts will make things right as high as they should be. A few hours later, an automated response arrived. A little while later, I received another automated reply: The representative hadn't found anything. He then returned my call, and I asked whether I had missed a step. He told me that all I needed to do was install the program and wait for a few days for the service to be activated. I downloaded and installed the product, and it worked. My contact was still the same person, and I spent about three minutes talking to him before he hung up. In less thanan hour, I'd had two support interactions. In this day and age, that's a good deal.

When you install Windows Defender Antivirus or Windows Defender Security Center, you also install Windows Defender Next-Generation Firewall. It's an entry-level firewall that's well worth installing.

You can start Windows Defender Next-Generation Firewall by selecting "Firewall," but you don't need to if you don't want to. It's your choice. In the Scan Mode dropdown menu (a second option is "Network & Internet Shield"), you can set the standard or high-level firewall for all network ports. To enable content filters, you must be running Windows 11 Enterprise, Enterprise E1, Enterprise E3, or Education edition. It also has a firewall setting for browsers, but you're much more likely to want to apply this setting.

Few applications rely entirely on the firewall to provide security, so you needn't take extra steps to make sure that they can connect and communicate securely. But if you have sensitive personal information, and you're using a browser to protect that information, make sure that it can't be tampered with. You also might want to change the default settings for all network ports. For example, I use Firefox, but I haven't yet changed the default to Internet Explorer. I don't expect to, but it's always good practice to learn how to do it. If you ever want to use another browser on your Windows 11 PC, you can change the default security settings.

Sharing your files is a reasonable worry, especially if you're not sure what your kids or guests will do with them. That's why Windows Defender Points lets you put files in "safe mode," in which they appear but won't be manipulated. This mode will show up when you right-click a file.

I like that Windows Defender Points doesn't require you to run the software in an elevated security mode. When you click Windows Defender Points, it opens the Security Center and displays a list of your networked Windows apps. If you want to share a file, the list will show a button labeled Share > Send to Windows Defender Points. Click this button, and a dialog box will pop up with an invitation to Send to Windows Defender Points. Click OK.

The sharing dialog shows you whether you've selected one or more files to share and provides buttons to share that file to both a particular folder in the user folder and all user folders. If you select all folders, Windows Defender Points displays the date and time that it was last copied to the remote server. For examp le, copying a file from the C: drive to a folder named "Documents" would make the file appear on the remote server.

Windows Defender Points can also display a link to a website that hosts malware, but you don't need to share that link with anyone. Windows Defender Points is a standalone product that you can install on your Windows 11 PC without altering other programs on the system.

Worried that someone might read your files and get into your kill all files? In one of my demos, a researcher took some proprietary information that he wanted to study, and with Windows Defender Next-Generation Firewall, he was able to copy it to his Windows 11 PC and edit it without fear of it being read by others.

Security and privacy features extend beyond the firewall and the new scanning options. A Windows Defender Security Center is always available, but you don't need to launch it manually. It's always on, so if you're logged into Windows, just hit Windows Defender Security Center on the taskbar.

If you want, you can click the link labeled "System Status" in the upper-right corner of the window and toggle the visibility of other notifications. The notification is one of the options available in the "Notifications" box on the left. If you click that notification, you get a list of security alerts from Windows Defender, Windows, Windows Defender Antivirus, Windows Defender Action Center, Windows Defender SmartScreen Filter, Windows Update, Windows Event Viewer, Windows Update Advanced Options, Windows Privacy Settings, Windows Search, and Windows Update Business.

You can click the category at the top of the list for the specific alerts that you want to see. For example, if you want to see all warnings, you can click the "Warnings" button.

I'm a big fan of the new version of Windows Defender. The new Scan option works well and is easy to use. The new firewall scans and blocks, without forcing you to jump through hoops. And you can now scan through all of Windows 11 without manually clicking individual items. All of these features could potentially be handy in the event of an attack. But if I were forced to judge, I'd have to give the edge to Kaspersky, our Editors' Choice for antivirus.

Users can install Windows Defender Applications. Although there isn't a Windows Defender security suite equivalent to Kaspersky's offering, the bundled programs make it easier for malware victims to get rid of their infections. The included Malware Protection Center is a better interface for scanning your PC than what Kaspersky offers, but it's far more complicated to use than the standalone Windows Defender Security Center.

How to Add Windows Defender to Your Desktop

To add Windows Defender to your desktop, go to Settings > Update & security > Windows Defender.

Here, you'll see a list of antivirus programs that you can install on your PC. If Windows Defender is already installed, Windows 11 will automatically install it and show a message to confirm you want it to stay. If it's not installed, you'll be shown a window to download the software and install it.

Click on the "Install" button to install Windows Defender on your PC. Once Windows Defender is installed, you can go back to Settings > Update & security > Windows Defender to make sure it's running.

There's no easy way to configure Windows Defender to automatically run when your PC starts, though. You have to either restart your PC or manually run Windows Defender.

What Is Windows Defender Antivirus?

For a long time, Microsoft was known for its bloatware, unwanted software with preloaded features, and high prices. Microsoft cleaned up a lot of that in the last few years, like the removal of Windows Media Player, but the reason Windows Defender is a new addition is because of the software update Microsoft released in 2014.

Windows Defender was previously called Windows Malicious Software Removal Tool (MSRT). MSRT had an annoying habit of taking over a Windows system, deactivating your primary antimalware software, and installing a plethora of "emergency" settings. MSRT was often found on MSDN (Microsoft's how-to site) and had a reputation for being fairly aggressive. As I wrote in 2015, I used MSRT for years, and one day the plug was pulled on it. Microsoft told me that MSRT had issues with ESRAM and a buggy update process, causing numerous reports to Windows. "We received the majority of your feedback privately and have reviewed it. As part of this review we had a dedicated team review all active software found on your PC, and today we are issuing a mandatory update to remove the offending software and related settings from your device. Effective immediately, Windows Defender Security Center is the only solution available to protect your Windows PC.

That's the basic version of the story. Microsoft implemented a ton of new features into Windows Defender in 2014, which is when Windows Defender Antivirus (WDASVAC) was born. Some of the features include the ability to add categories of security threats for your antimalware protection to see updates for, some new automatic security scans (to make it more efficient), and some new diagnostic tools.

Windows Defender now has four main components, which are the Antivirus component, Real-Time Protection component, Malicious Software Removal Tool component, and the Toolbox. The Antivirus component has three differen t tiers— Web, Desktop, and Mobile. The web is designed to detect and stop websites that show security warnings when you go to the site. It has a SmartSearch feature to quickly pinpoint web-based threats, and it blocks malicious downloads on Windows Store apps. Desktop is designed for users who use Microsoft Office and see lots of security warnings, so it blocks more types of malware. And finally, the Mobile component is for anyone who downloads malware to their device and sees lots of warnings. This is the most limited antivirus solution I've seen, so the firewall and browser cleaning are gone.

WDASVAC can also perform some system health checks, like scanning for software faults or unoptimized drivers. It can also protect your laptop, phone, or tablet from malicious apps, since the Antivirus component is responsible for that, and it does a whole bunch of reporting to alert you to risks and for troubleshooting. The Toolbox part is only available with Windows 11 Enterprise, and it includes important features like a compressed file viewer, software updater, and password manager.

It's not like it's hard to block malware, but the problem is that most consumers don't know that they have malware. You'd have to have malware on your PC, but chances are your Windows Defender package hasn't found any, and even if it did, it wouldn't be available for removal. And if you're a non-enterprise user, Microsoft will also warn you that it can't do anything about the problem, and you'll need to contact the manufacturer for help.

But, as with any antivirus program, you'll need to install driver updates and some antivirus software. Typically you can just click on a link, it'll check your PC for malware, and you're good to go. But while there is a link in Windows 11, you'll need to click and then enter a password to have the link show up in your settings.

Is it fair to say that Windows Defender is an antivirus? The truth is that it's an antivirus, but it also acts as a scanner. And a more truth would be to say that Windows Defender is an antivirus, but doesn't do everything you could need an antivirus to do.

Those who aren't installing antivirus software, however, can't use Windows Defender to protect themselves. And it doesn't help that Windows Defender is more of a bug - checking machine than a malware-stopping one.

At its core, the best way to prevent malware is to install a decent antivirus on your PC. But you should know that most of the top antivirus suites are free, as are a lot of the best antivirus scanning programs.

To help you compare antivirus suites, PCMag.com provides a PCMag.com Security Scorecard, which ranks security suites by risk, detection, and protection, evaluating a suite's ability to block ransomware and other malware. Our favorite two suites, Bitdefender and Kaspersky, were among the best we tested.

Antivirus: Core, Basic, and Safe (contains malware-fighting components)

Windows Defender Antivirus is very good at detecting and removing malware, but it also relies on the same scanning capabilities that your browser uses to make sure that the sites you're visiting are safe.

Microsoft can't run the malware-killing component, but if you enable Windows Defender's SmartScreen filter it does automatically clean up malware-ridden sites. The SmartScreen filter relies on a Microsoft scanning engine, so the two won't work in concerts like Bitdefender and Kaspersky.

For an extra layer of protection, you can pay a bit more for a Windows Defender security suite, which is the version that comes with Windows 11. Windows Defender Security Center is a great way to see all of your software security options in one place. And, yes, you can pay for a Windows Defender subscription, which includes SmartScreen filtering, though a free trial is also available.

Antivirus Protection

One change in Windows 11 is a significant one: in previous versions, Windows Defender ran in the background while users used the operating system. However, as the name implies, it was also supposed to offer some kind of antiphishing protection. In Windows 10, Windows Defender Antivirus was optional and was activated only if users explicitly enabled it. The new Windows 11 version of Windows Security Essentials includes an antiphishing feature called Windows Defender Antivirus that is activated when Windows Defender Antivirus is installed, but it's based on Active Protection Service technology from Bitdefender.

Antivirus technology in Windows Defender Antivirus isn't exactly new. In Windows 10, it used the same technology as Windows Defender Antivirus, and in Windows 10 it used the same technology as Windows Defender Antivirus Pro. The difference in Windows 11 is that Windows Defender Antivirus uses Bitdefender's Active Protection Service and can detect and remove malware when it runs. This is similar to how Microsoft's own Windows Defender Antivirus works, and it should provide stronger anti-malware protection than anything that might be installed by users if they choose to do so themselves. Bitdefender's tech also supports self-protection against ransomware and other forms of malware.

Bitdefender's Active Protection Service can also automatically detect and block malware on a more local basis. When you install a program, the system can generate an event log for that program that includes information about how the program was executed and information about other files and processes that the program was interacting with. It can then highlight any of these processes that were modified by malware during that execution and remove the modified files automatically, without having to perform a full scan. This feature was part of Windows Defender Antivirus in previous versions, and it's now included in Windows 11.

Windows Defender Antivirus also includes support for third-party security solutions, much like Windows Defender AntiVirus in Windows 10. This means that if you install Windows Defender Antivirus or Windows Defender Antivirus Pro, you can use them to secure your browsers and other system resources. If you don't install Windows Defender Antivirus or Windows Defender Antivirus Pro, however, Windows Defender Antivirus continues to work in a similar manner to its predecessors. This is helpful for people who don't want to spend time removing built - in features when they no longer need them.

It used to be common for people to stick with traditional antivirus software that also had other functions, like firewall and phishing protection. When Windows XP debuted in 2001, one of the big updates for that operating system was a free PC antivirus called AVG. It was a rather skimpy software suite and had more in common with free Mac antivirus software than anything else. As such, it had a bad reputation with many Windows users. (It still does to a degree.)

Microsoft purchased AVG for $7.6 billion in 2015. In July 2018, the company renamed it Microsoft Security Essentials. It's still Windows-only software, but it now has stronger, more robust malware detection and removal features.

All Windows 11 users, regardless of whether or not they opt to use Microsoft Security Essentials, can benefit from Microsoft's Windows Defender Windows Security app, which collects threat intelligence to detect and block potential threats. You can also have Windows Defender automatically install when Windows 11 starts, so it's always available if you need it. It works with any Windows 11 PC.

There are other third-party antivirus software options for Windows, but if you don't want to deal with managing software updates and subscriptions, Microsoft Security Essentials is your best bet.

The Windows Defender website has a great FAQ section about how it can be used to protect against viruses, phishing, and other online threats.

Other Options

There are also third-party security products that combine antivirus scanning with malware-fighting technologies. These products tend to be more robust than the free alternatives, and many of them include plug-ins that enable remote control of your computer.

McAfee's suite of security tools includes McAfee Total Protection, which includes a network security scanner, Windows Defender, and the company's VPN service. The Total Protection Edition also includes McAfee Antivirus for Mac, though there's a similar product for Mac called McAfee Total Protection.

Dell's Security Essentials comes with two hardware-based features that integrate with your antivirus program to defend your computer: antivirus protection and remote device access protection. This suite can also protect your Android phone and iPad, and the Windows versions of the tools integrate with the Microsoft account service, meaning that the products work well with both Windows and Mac systems.

Webroot SecureAnywhere AntiVirus offers a lot of protection at a bargain price. $59.95 gets you web browsing protection, malware scanning, social media protection, banking protection, and a WebAdvisor feature that scans URLs for potential threats before you load them.

ESET Internet Security brings a comprehensive antivirus engine with features like VPN, antispamprotection, and anti-theft. This is one of the best-selling security suites out there, and it doesn't cost a cent, but it also has a pricey Plus edition, which adds parental control features, parental archive recovery, and antispam.

Avast Free Antivirus is perhaps the best-known name in antivirus, and while it's very good at basic antivirus tasks, it doesn't include malware-protecting technologies like SmartScreen, SmartClean, or McAfee.

Panda Free Antivirus includes a load of protection: malicious URL filtering, antivirus, malware scanning, social media protection, secure surfing, and firewall p rotection.

How to Connect and Extend to an External Display

This segment will go through connecting and extending your display to a second display device in Windows 11. It comes in handy if you have a second monitor or a TV where you want to project to or if you want to connect to a projector in a classroom or a business meeting. So typically, as soon as you connect a second monitor to your PC, by default, the content from your main PC will be mirrored to the second one. That's referred to as the mirror display.

Now to connect to a projector, press the Windows key on the keyboard, then press the letter p on the keyboard, and it will bring up the menu below.

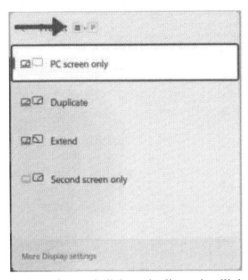

So if you have a second monitor and click on duplicate, it will duplicate the screen, and typically by default, it will be duplicated as soon as you connect a second screen.

However, another function that you need to use is the extended desktop. That will make you move the mouse from one screen to another and open one application and another on the other screen. To do that, click on the extend display option. The way you get to these options is by pressing the Windows key and then the letter P.

Now, if, for some reason, you don't remember the Windows key and P for a project, one of the things that you can do is click on the Start menu. On the search icon, type extends if you want to extend the desktop, type the Word duplicate and click on duplicate or extend. It will give you the options for multiple displays and so on.

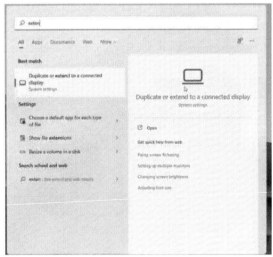

How to Connect to a Windows PC and Mirror the Screen from an Android Device

Windows 11 can allow other devices to mirror the screen from the remote device to Windows 11 device. It is done using the projection tool in combination with the connect tool. That is typically done with a Miracast connection which is a Microsoft technology available through Android devices. The devices have to be on the same Wireless Network and support the Miracast connection for this to work.

To do this, go to Windows search on your taskbar, then search for projection. In your projection settings, enable the options to allow Windows and android devices to project to the PC. So you'd have to approve it, but yet you should make your computer available. This availability is for you to connect both from an android device or a Windows PC.

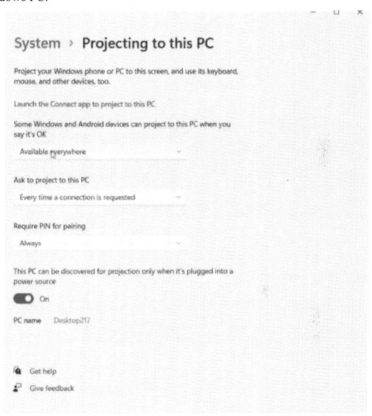

So next is to make sure that you approve the connection every time a connection is requested. Then the third one is to provide a pin. You can say never to it, and as soon as you confirm it, it will be able to connect, or you can give your pin every time to connect.

There are additional help options at the bottom as well. But once you are ready for someone to connect to your PC, you'd click "launch the connect app to project to the

PC," which will make your computer available for someone to connect. It will make the computer a discoverable Network to connect.

Now on the android devices, go to settings, select Cast, broadcasting, mirror, or connect, depending on the type of phone you are using. You might have to look through the settings to connect or mirror your screen to another device. It's important to note that this function will not work on Apple devices. So once you're ready to allow a connection, click on launch. The Connect app will project to your PC.

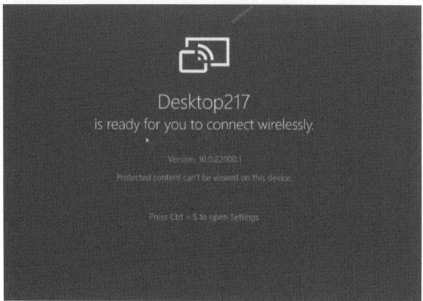

So when it connects, you'll see the content or mirror of their screen. On the device, select connect to a remote device. You either use the cast option on your PC, windows + K, on the keyboard, or connect to a remote display. Depending on the android model, you would have to use the connect or mirror option in an android device.

How to Cast or Connect to An External Device

This section will look into casting or connecting to an external device, remote monitor, remote TV, or a remote Windows PC. So Windows 11 has the functionality to connect to a remote display, and you can do that by simply pressing the Windows key and then the letter k. That will bring up the cast option.

If you don't remember pressing the Windows key and then k, you can go under the search option on the taskbar and then type in Cast in the search bar. Then you have the option to connect to a wireless display, then click on connect. It will bring you back to the same option that you have with the shortcut method.

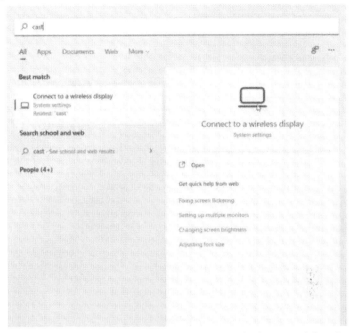

One other option is to go to quick action items on the bottom right of your home screen. You can click on any of those icons at the bottom to add other functionality such as the nearby sharing, casting, or projection to add the project icon to always access it easily. Add it once, and then you're done. When you go in the future and click on quick actions instead of having to do control k or Windows P, you will immediately have the option to cast or project from the quick action.

How to Connect to a Windows PC and Mirror the Screen from an Android Device

Windows 11 can allow other devices to mirror the screen from the remote device to Windows 11 device. It is done using the projection tool in combination with the connect tool. That is typically done with a Miracast connection which is a Microsoft technology available through Android devices. The devices have to be on the same Wireless Network and support the Miracast connection for this to work.

To do this, go to Windows search on your taskbar, then search for projection. In your projection settings, enable the options to allow Windows and android devices to project to the PC. So you'd have to approve it, but yet you should make your computer available. This availability is for you to connect both from an android device or a Windows PC.

System › Projecting to this PC

Project your Windows phone or PC to this screen, and use its keyboard, mouse, and other devices, too.

Launch the Connect app to project to this PC

Some Windows and Android devices can project to this PC when you say it's OK

Available everywhere ⌄

Ask to project to this PC

Every time a connection is requested ⌄

Require PIN for pairing

Always ⌄

This PC can be discovered for projection only when it's plugged into a power source

⬤ On

PC name   Desktop217

🔍 Get help

💬 Give feedback

So next is to make sure that you approve the connection every time a connection is requested. Then the third one is to provide a pin. You can say never to it, and as soon as you confirm it, it will be able to connect, or you can give your pin every time to connect.

There are additional help options at the bottom as well. But once you are ready for someone to connect to your PC, you'd click "launch the connect app to project to the PC," which will make your computer available for someone to connect. It will make the computer a discoverable Network to connect.

Now on the android devices, go to settings, select Cast, broadcasting, mirror, or connect, depending on the type of phone you are using. You might have to look through the settings to connect or mirror your screen to another device. It's important to note that this function will not work on Apple devices. So once you're ready to allow a connection, click on launch. The Connect app will project to your PC.

Desktop217
is ready for you to connect wirelessly.

Version: 10.0.22000.1

Protected content can't be viewed on this device.

Press Ctrl + & to open Settings

So when it connects, you'll see the content or mirror of their screen. On the device, select connect to a remote device. You either use the cast option on your PC, windows + K, on the keyboard, or connect to a remote display. Depending on the android model, you would have to use the connect or mirror option in an android device.

Working with Fonts in Windows 11

Downloading and Installing Fonts Manually in Windows 11

There are a lot of fonts included with Windows 11 and they can be found in the C:/Windows/Fonts directory. You can still download and install more fonts if you are unhappy with these fonts. Newly installed fonts can also be used in applications, including the operating system and office. For the most part, fonts are packaged in zip files, which means they have to be unzipped before they can be used.

If you wish to download fonts, go to any website of your choice, download the font you like the most, and then extract the file because it is a zip file. You can then select a font from a drop-down menu.

It's important to note that the Microsoft Store is the easiest way for most Windows users to install new fonts since it's a straightforward process likely to avoid installing anything malicious on your system, which isn't guaranteed when you're installing a font from an obscure website. Using the Microsoft Store, here's how you can install new fonts on Windows 11.

1. Visit the *Microsoft Store*. Windows 11 automatically pins the Microsoft Store to the Taskbar and Start menu, but if you remove them, you can find it by searching for "*Microsoft Store*" on the Start menu.

2. Use the top search bar to find '*Fonts.*' "Fonts" should appear at the top of the results menu. If it's not, you can tell because it's got a nondescript icon that says "Explore new fonts." Click it.

3. Click on the '*Explore new fonts*' button. There are numerous fonts on this page that Microsoft designed itself, and it devotes a lot of space to them.

4. Select a font you like

   Here all you need to do is pick whichever option catches your eye.

5. Click the '*Free*' button

   The Microsoft Store doesn't even require you to create an account to use free fonts; simply click the "Free" button. For paid fonts, you will need a Microsoft account and a payment method before you can confirm your purchase and install the font.

6. Locate the downloaded font

   If you saved the font somewhere else, you can either navigate to the appropriate folder in File Explorer or use Windows 11's search tool to find it.

7. (Optional) Decompress the file

Downloaded fonts can be extracted from ZIP files by right-clicking, selecting "Extract All..." and click "Extract" in the dialog box that appears. For .rar files, additional software is necessary.

8. Select the files you need. Many fonts ship with numerous font faces (bold, italic, etc.) and weights (light, heavy, and so on) you can use. If you want to install all of them for posterity's sake, you can select all of them. If you only want to install a few of them, just pick the ones you need, and ignore the rest.

9. Right-click and, if the option to install doesn't appear, select 'Show more options' in the menu. Windows 11 has removed the ability to install fonts by right-clicking the appropriate file and then choosing the appropriate option, so you'll have to click "Show more options" or press Shift+F10 to access it.

10. Select the option for *'Install'* or *'Install for all users'* from the menu. The fonts can be installed by normal users, but they must be installed for every account in the system. Either way, once you click the appropriate option, a progress window should appear that automatically closes once the font has been successfully installed.

Activate the Font File

Users should see two buttons at the top left of the window once it has been opened: *'Print' and 'Install.'* Install your new font and make use of it.

How can I change the primary monitor?

Display

Windows HD Color settings

Scale and layout

Change the size of text, apps, and other items

100% (Recommended) ∨

Advanced scaling settings

Display resolution

1366 × 768 (Recommended) ∨

Display orientation

Landscape ∨

Multiple displays

Older displays might not always connect automatically. Select Detect to try to connect to them.

Advanced display settings

Graphics settings

So, you want to change your main monitor in Windows 11, but owing to the changes in the new OS, you don't know how to accomplish it. Don't worry; these are all the steps you'll need to complete the task and have your combat station up and running the way you want it.

<u>Display Options</u>

If you're experiencing difficulties with the PC recognizing the monitor, you'll need to perform a little debugging.

Troubleshoot First of all, you need to check if you plugged the cord into the correct port. Windows will allow you to run two different GPUs at the same time, like NVIDIA and Intel.

For now, disconnect the gadget from the motherboard and into the GPU. Most GPUs don't have two HDMI connections, thus you may need to fit in with either a USB-C cable (in the slot meant for VR) or a Display Port cable.

Note: If you're still experiencing problems after doing this, try hitting the Windows Key + P. This will bring up the monitor quick settings, which may have it configured to display just one screen at a time. If it does not s till work for a second time, try another cable.

The final major option is to update your graphics card drivers, as well as the onboard graphics card supplied with Intel-based motherboards, by going to Device Manager (Search > Device Manager).

If you wish to do it via Device Manager, right-click on the device and choose Update Driver from the menu that appears.

Monitor Menu

Now that you're in the menu, it'll show you your two or more monitors, along with an estimate of their size and placement concerning how you will move your mouse between them. You can not only move your displays around and slide the icons around, but you can also accomplish what you arrived for:

The main display is being replaced.

Click the icon for the monitor you wish to use as your primary display, and everything will nearly always load on that screen first from now on.

Helpful Inclusion in Windows 11

The new feature in Windows 11 is that if you detach a monitor, it will try to remember where various application windows were. This is excellent news for laptop users who move from a dock or cable connection to another location since when you return to the setup, you will be right where you left off without having to reorganize yourself for five minutes after Windows has played 52-card-pick-up with your desktop.

How to install Fonts via Settings in Windows 11 or 10

Locate your downloaded font Locate your downloaded font Navigate to the 'Personalization' page in Settings; Select the 'Fonts' option. ...

Drag your downloaded font to the appropriate box in Settings Confirm the font was installed.

Windows 11 Shortcuts Keys, Tips and Tricks

As a reminder, below are the newly added shortcut keys

Action	Shortcut
Opening Action Center	Win + A
Opening Notifications Panel (Notification Center)	Win + N
Opening Widgets Panel	Win + W
Quick Access to Snap Layout	Win + Z
Open Microsoft Teams	Win + C

Action	Shortcut
Turn on Magnifier and Zoom	Win + plus (+)
Zoom out using Magnifier	Win + minus (-)
Open "Ease of Access" Centre in Windows Settings	Win + U
Exit Magnifier	Win + Esc
Switch to the docked mode in Magnifier	Alt + Ctrl + D
Switch to full-screen mode in Magnifier	Alt + Ctrl + F
Turn Sticky Keys on or off	Press Shift five times
Switch to lens mode in Magnifier	Alt + Ctrl + L
Invert colors in Magnifier	Alt + Ctrl + I
Cycle through views in Magnifier	Alt + Ctrl + M
Resize the lens with the mouse in Magnifier	Alt + Ctrl + R
Pan in Magnifier	Alt + Ctrl + Arrow keys
Zoom in or out	Ctrl + Alt + mouse scroll
Open Narrator	Win + Enter
Turn Toggle Keys on or off	Press Num Lock for five seconds
Open on-screen keyboard with this shortcut in Windows 11	Win + Ctrl + O
Turn Filter Keys on and off	Hold down Right Shift for eight seconds
Turn High Contrast on or off	Left Alt + Left Shift + PrtSc

Turn Mouse Keys on or off	Left Alt + Left Shift + Num Lock

Tips and Tricks

Upgrading Windows 10 to Windows 11

In general, Microsoft made the upgrading process to Windows 10 surprisingly simple, so we're expecting an even smoother version as the actual launch date approaches.

Is it free to upgrade from Windows 10 to Windows 11?

In reality, no one knows the precise features at this early stage, but we can guess, and we are projecting, that, similar to Windows 8 to Windows 10, there will be a free upgrade route initially at least to encourage take-up.

When a new operating system is released into the wild, maintaining older systems becomes more difficult. As far as Microsoft is concerned, the more people who upgrade to Windows 11 the better.

There are references to the update being free on Microsoft's website, but there hasn't been an outright press statement on the subject yet, so we're not sure whether there are any restrictions.

Start the PC Health Checker

Double-click the downloaded application. When you run this application, you'll learn not only about your PC but also whether it's ready for Windows 11 when the time comes. Many people are reporting that the tool is telling them that their computer isn't capable of running Windows 11, but we're confident that this will be resolved soon.

How to Factory Reset Windows 11

To factory reset your Windows 11 computer, click the **start** button and then select Settings. You can also press **Windows + I** on your keyboard to open the Settings app. Navigate to the System tab, then select the **Recovery** option. Select **Reset PC** from the Recovery Settings section. You will see the following window when you click Reset PC.

Keep my files: if you want to keep all of your files intact while the system apps are uninstalled and system settings are rolled back to a fresh state.

Remove everything: This option will remove everything (photos, programs, and apps)and roll back the OS to a fresh state.

Follow the prompts to reset your computer after selecting the option that fit s your needs best.

Basic Troubleshooting

Just like everything else in life, nothing works perfectly all the time, and that goes for computers and Windows as well. But if you learn some basic troubleshooting skills, you can fix a lot of the common problems you may encounter as you use your computer on a regular basis.

Strange Characters (Gibberish) Being Printed on the Page

Check your printer property settings under the Advanced tab to make sure the right driver is being used.

Error Messages, Crashes, and Freezing Issues

There are many reasons why a computer can crash, freeze, reboot itself, and so on. Sometimes it's easy to figure out the problem, and sometimes it is very difficult. Poorly written software can cause crashes because of conflicts with oth er programs, shared files, and compatibility issues with Windows itself. Hardware can cause crashes as well, mostly because of buggy device drivers which the software used to allow the hardware to work with Windows.

The computer's hardware itself can cause issues because if there is a problem with essential hardware (such as the processor or RAM), then Windows will not run properly, if at all. Even something as simple as your processor getting hot can cause issues and crashes. Computer hardware doesn't last forever, even though it seems that if it's going to go bad it will happen sooner rather than later.

Error Types

There are many types of errors you can receive on your computer, which makes it even harder to narrow down the cause sometimes.

Application errors – These can be caused by faulty software in regard to how it was created\programmed. They can also happen because of an unexplained glitch in the software, a compatibility error with other software, or with Windows itself.

System errors – When you see these you can assume it's related to a Windows problem, or maybe even a hardware or driver issue. Many times a reboot will clear up these types of errors.

Stop errors – These are usually caused by faulty hardware such as bad RAM or a bad sector on your hard drive. When you see these errors, you are usually looking at the famous Blue Screen of Death (discussed next) message on your monitor.

POST errors – POST (Power on Self Test) errors can be caused by faulty hardware or BIOS\motherboard misconfigurations. You usually hear a beep sequence on boot up, and then you can research the beep pattern to help narrow down the problem.

Runtime errors – These are usually caused by corrupt application executables or system files that cause certain programs to shut themselves down, or not even open to begin with. Sometimes they can even cause your computer to freeze up.

Windows Blue Screen of Death (BSOD)

If you have been using Microsoft Windows for a while, there is most likely a chance you have encountered a blue screen of death error. This is where the computer will simply crash in the middle of whatever you are doing, and the screen will be a blue background with white text (figure 11.6) showing the error and some suggestions as to what the cause can be. Many times you can look up the hex values that say something similar to 0xF73120AE to get an idea of the cause. If you are lucky, you can reboot and carry on, but sometimes the BSOD will occur again right after you reboot. BSOD errors are usually caused by faulty hardware or poorly written device driver software and can be very difficult to diagnose.

```
***STOP: 0x000000D1 (0x00000000, 0xF73120AE, 0xC0000008, 0xC0000000)

A problem has been detected and Windows has been shut down to prevent damage
to your computer

DRIVER_IRQL_NOT_LESS_OR_EQUAL

If this is the first time you've seen this Stop error screen, restart your
computer. If this screen appears again, follow these steps:

Check to make sure any new hardware or software is properly installed. If this is a
new installation, ask your hardware or software manufacturer for any windows updates
you might need.

If problems continue, disable or remove any newly installed hardware or software.
Disable BIOS memory options such as caching or shadowing. If you need to use Safe
Mode to remove or disable components, restart your computer, press F8 to select
Advanced Startup Options, and then select Safe Mode.

****  ABCD.SYS - Address F73120AE base at C0000000, DateStamp 368072A3

Kernel Debugger Using: COM2 (Port 0x2F8, Baud Rate 19200)
Beginning dump of physical memory
Physical memory dump complete. Contact your system administrator or
technical support group.
```

Use your old applications as well as new, better applications,

- Effective from Windows 11, Windows Insiders may utilize the Microsoft Store to install and download Android applications. The Android Windows Subsystem is a functionality that lets you utilize Android applications on your Windows systems in the same way that you can use applications from the Microsoft Store.

  You go to the Microsoft Store, download the Amazon Appstore application, and log in using your Amazon credentials. Then search for, install, and download Android applications after logging in.

- Your Windows 10 applications will run on Windows 11. If there're any problems, the application Assure is also accessible.

For your WinForm, WPF, Wind32, and UWP desktop files, you can keep using MSIX files. To download and deploy Windows programs, keep using Windows Package Manager. To modularize apps and desktops, utilize Azure Virtual Desktop plus MSIX application attach.

You can modify various applications settings in the Settings app > Apps. You can obtain software from any place, for instance, but you should let the company know if there is a similar application in the Microsoft Store. You may also select which applications launch when you log in.

You can define policies that govern some application settings with an MDM service such as Endpoint Manager.

If you use Endpoint Manager to oversee your devices, you're probably already acquainted with the Company Portal software. The Company Portal, which debuted with Windows 11, is a secret application store for your institution's applications.

Windows Terminal Application This software comes pre-installed with the operating system. It's a distinct downloadable in the Microsoft Store for older Windows editions.

Within that command prompt, this program integrates Azure Cloud Shell, a command prompt, and Windows PowerShell. To utilize these command-line programs, you do not need to launch any other applications. There are tabs on it. You may also pick your command-line program when you start a fresh tab: Employ policy to bring the Windows Terminal application to the Taskbar or Start menu layout if groups of people in your business often use the command prompt or Windows PowerShell.

Also, you can find the Terminal software by searching for it, right -clicking it, and pinning it to the taskbar and Start menu.

- The Microsoft Store now has a redesigned appearance and now contains a larger selection of retail and public applications.

- The default browser is the Microsoft Edge browser, which is integrated with the operating system. In Windows 11, Internet Explorer isn't accessible. If a webpage requires Internet Explorer, you can utilize Internet Explorer Mode in Microsoft Edge. Launch the Microsoft Edge browser and input edge:/settings/defaultBrowser inside the space provided for URLs.

Microsoft Edge employs sleeping tabs in saving system resources. Edge:/settings/systemallows you to customize these and other configurations.

You can customize some Microsoft Edge setup with an MDM vendor like Endpoint Manager or even Group Policy.

Servicing and Deployment

- *Install Windows 11*: You can install Windows 11 using the same techniques you employed in installing Windows 10.

You may use Microsoft Deployment Toolkit, Configuration Manager, Windows Autopilot, and other tools to deploy Windows to your devices. Windows 11 will be available as a free update to qualified Windows 10 machines.

- *Windows Autopilot*: If you are buying a new gadget, Windows Autopilot can help you set them up and configure them. Users check-in with their company account (user@contoso.com) when they receive the gadget.

Autopilot prepares items for usage in the backdrop and runs any applications or policies you specify. Windows Autopilot may also be used to reset, reuse, and restore devices. Admins can implement Autopilot with zero effort.

If you've got a worldwide or virtual workforce, Autopilot may be the best solution for installing and setting up the operating system.

- Microsoft Endpoint Manager is a supplier of mobile device management and mobile app management. It aids in the management of apps and devices on those devices in your company. You create policies and then distribute them to users and organizations. You may use policies to install applications, set device functionalities, impose PIN needs, and prevent hacked devices, among other things.

If you're already using Group Policy to control Windows 10 endpoints, you could use it to operate Windows 11 gadgets as well. Most of these policies are available in Endpoint Manager's settings catalog and administrative templates. G n -premises group policy items that are on-premised are analyzed using group policy insights.

- Manage features and updates on your endpoints using Delivery Optimization and Windows Updates. The operating system feature patches are downloaded and deployed once a year beginning with Windows 11.

Windows 11 will get monthly quality improvements, much the same as Windows 10.

Windows Server Update Services, Group Policy, Endpoint Managers, and more tools are available to help you apply upgrades on your Windows systems. Some upgrades are enormous in size and consume a lot of data.

Delivery optimization aids in the reduction of data use. It distributes the task of obtaining the update files among your deployment's many endpoints. Windows 11 patches are smaller since they just download new source files. Policies that define delivery optimization parameters can be created. Specify the maximum download and upload bandwidth, as well as cache sizes and other options.

How to Clone HDD to SSD in Windows 11

In light of Microsoft's decision to make Windows 11 the next -generation operating system, you're probably looking forward to installing Windows 11 on your SSD rather than your hard drive. Due to SSD's increased speed and compact size, they are always recommended to install operating systems.

However, there is a bit of preparation that needs to take place before Windows 11 can be migrated to SSD. This includes:

- Take a backup of your SSD before formatting.

- Check that your SSD is connected to your PC or laptop, whether it's via a USB to SATA adapter, or if it's in a disk bay within your cabinet (for desktop PCs).

- Ensure that the SSD drive is recognized under the Devices & drives section of This PC.

Make sure your new drive is ready

It is necessary to prepare a new hard drive or preferably an SSD with more capacity to clone Windows 11. Make sure the hard drive or SSD you will use for cloning has more storage space than your existing drive.

Using Task Manager and Ctrl-Alt-Del

One of the tools you will become familiar with when learning how to troubleshoot your computer is called *Task Manager*. This tool is used for a variety of different things, from monitoring performance to killing unresponsive programs.

To open Task Manager, you can do a search for it, or you can press *Ctrl-Alt-Del* on your keyboard and then choose Task Manager from the menu items. Many times, if your computer is not responding to mouse input, you have to use the Ctrl-Alt-Del method. The purpose of Ctrl-Alt-Del is to be sure that you are typing your password into a real login form and not some other fake process trying to steal your password and to also restart the computer if needed. Once you have Task Man ager open, you can click on More details at the lower left of the window and then you will see a window with multiple tabs such as Process, Performance and App history.

Now I will briefly go over what all the tabs in Task Manager are used for so you hav ea basic understanding of what you can do with it.

Processes – Shows the running processes on the computer and what percentage of CPU, memory, disk, *etc.* is being used by that process. Processes are instances of an executable (.exe) used to run programs. If you have a program that is not responding, you can highlight it and then click the "End task" button to force close the program. You can also right click the program and go to the actual location of the running executable file.

Performance – This tab shows the CPU, memory, disk, Ethernet, Bluetooth, Wi-Fi, and GPU total usage. You can click on each one and get real time usage graphs as well.

App history – Here you can see what apps were recently used and what resources they have consumed.

Startup – This tab shows you what programs are set to run every time you start your computer. (This topic will be discussed further when we get to the MSconfig tool in the next section.)

Users – If you have multiple users logged on to your computer, then you can get information about what resources and programs they are using from here. You can also disconnect remote users from here.

176

Details – Here you will find information such as the process ID, status, CPU usage, and memory for running programs. You can also see what user account is running the program, as well as a description of the process.

Services – This tab shows you all the installed services running on your computer and their running state.

System Configuration Utility (MSconfig)

The Windows System Configuration utility (also commonly known as MSconfig since that's what most people type in the search or run box to open it) has been around for many years and is still a valuable tool for troubleshooting.

When you open the System Configuration utility, you will notice that it has several tabs just like Task Manager does. Once again, we will go over what each tab does so you can get an idea of how the System Configuration utility can help you manage and troubleshoot your computer. The easiest way to open this tool is to type *msconfig* in the search box.

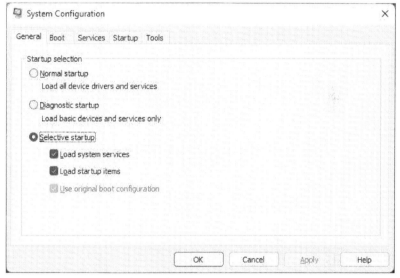

General – Here you can choose how you want your computer to start up when it comes to device drivers and services. *Normal* will load all drivers and services, *diagnostic* will load only the basic drivers and services, and *selective* will let you choose what services and startup items are loaded. The default is Normal, but the Normal startup option changes to Selective startup if you select any of the options in the Advanced Troubleshooting Settings dialog box.

Boot – This tab lets you decide what operating system to load if you have more than one installed on your computer. The Boot options section lets you choose how your computer boots. So, if you want to do some diagnostics or testing, you can choose *Safe boot* and choose what options to load with it. Safe boot is the same thing as booting into Safe Mode, where you would press F8 on startup to load a basic configuration of Windows. Just be sure to change it back to normal after you are done so it won't go into Safe Mode on your next reboot. You can also change the timeout setting from the default of thirty seconds so it will load the default operating system faster if you have more than one.

Services – Just like Task Manager, MSconfig has a Services tab, but here you can enable and disable services, so they start or don't start with Windows. This comes in handy for diagnosing issues, and if you have some services that don't need to start every time with Windows, you can disable them to improve your computer's performance. (Just be sure that you know what the service does before you enable or disable it.)

Startup – In older versions of Windows, this would be where you would see what programs are set to run when Windows starts, but in Windows 10 it just shows a link to open Task Manager, and it will take you to the Startup tab there. This is one of the most commonly used areas because it allows you to prevent software from starting up that doesn't need to run every time you boot your computer, saving you resources an d also allowing the computer to start faster. Virus and spyware infections love to put items in your startup section so they will load every time you start your computer. So, if you are having a virus or spyware issue, this should be one of the first places you check to see if there is anything set to run that shouldn't be running, and then you can disable it.

Tools – This tab will let you run a variety of common tools all from one location. Some of these tools include Task Manager, System Restore, and Event Viewer. You can open all these tools from their default location, but it's nice to be able to see them all in one place. Plus, you may even discover a tool you didn't know existed.

Conclusion

Thank you for reading this book. Windows has always existed to serve as a platform for global innovation. It has served as the backbone of multinational companies and as the platform upon which scrappy startups have grown into household brands. Windows is where the web was born and grown. It's where many of us first sent an email, played our first PC game, and coded our first line. Windows is the platform on which people create, connect, learn, and accomplish—a platform on which over a billion people depend today.

What made this so effective was the transformation of the PC we saw and felt—from something utilitarian and functional to something personal and emotional. This is what motivated us to create the next version of Windows. To provide a familiar space for you to create, learn, play, and most importantly, connect in new ways.

When Windows 11 is released to the public, the Windows release health hub will include key servicing-related notifications as well as information regarding known problems and safeguard holds. At that time, a unified Windows 11 update h istory website will also have monthly release notes accessible.

With this new update and probably future updates as well, owning a Windows PC now seems to be a luxury. Its glassy feel along with its very easy-operation remains unchanged even though a lot of new features have been added to it. The ability to create new exciting features while still keeping the whole Operating system very simple is one reason why Windows users all over the world will always love Windows.

You have learned all the lessons and steps to undertake to maximize your use of the world's most recent Operating System on your PC. You can start using the Windows 11 with full confident and enjoy the most popular operating system in the world for PCs. Now you can tackle all the issues associated with Windows 11 and the lessons will always be relevant for you because, Windows 11 will be continuously upgraded to take main frame as Microsoft is set to end the support of Windows 10, and all the foundation for navigating and maximizing the new operating system has been comprehensively covered.

Now you have no limitation as far as the knowledge and the use of windows 11 is concerned. You can now get things done effectively like an expert with your windows 11 and can always run back to check whatever you didn't get from first reading.

With Windows 11, you are assured of getting the latest features, functions, and past tasks included in it. Like mentioned earlier, the release of the new Windows 11 will allow users to carry out certain functions including cloning HDD to SSD, pinning and unpinning apps in the start menu, managing disk space, customizing the Windows 11 start menu and so much more.

At a period where technology is a central part of human existence and interaction, Windows 11 is designed to make work even better. And now, with the emergence of Windows 11, it is glaring the improvements and the difference. This guide aims to analyze Windows 11 and paint a transparent picture to the user, enabling them to see the upgrade in its entirety and being able to follow the steps in their use of the upgrade.

Additionally, Windows 11 will get monthly quality upgrades, much like Windows 10. It will also have a fresh feature update schedule. Once a year, a feature update for Windows 11 will be issued.

While it satisfied the bulk of Windows users, the new Windows 11 was somewhat uninteresting to some other users. The elimination of some applications and functionalities and the redesign wasn't something they were particularly interested in. Windows 11 cuts through complexity and helps you focus on what's important.

Before the official release, coverage of Windows 11 revolved around the operating system's tighter hardware requirements, with arguments over whether they were actually intended to enhance Windows security or merely a trick to upsell users to newer devices, and also concerns over electronic waste related with the changes. When it was first released, Windows 11 was embraced for its advanced visual design, OS management, and security focus, but it was derided for backtracks and changes to the user interface.

Good luck.

ALPHABETICAL INDEX

A

Access, 9, 14, 20, 25, 28, 30, 36, 38, 44, 45, 48, 50, 51, 52, 54, 57, 74, 76, 89, 93, 98, 100, 103, 107, 108, 111, 112, 113, 116, 118, 120, 126, 140, 142, 143, 144, 151, 152, 154, 159, 163, 167

Account, 20, 32, 44, 45, 51, 90, 92, 93, 104, 116, 128, 130, 132, 140, 146, 147, 148, 149, 150, 151, 152, 153, 159, 166, 167, 174, 177

Android apps, 12, 17, 97, 128, 130

Antivirus, 140, 153, 154, 155, 156, 157, 158, 159

Apple, 146, 162, 164

Applications, 9, 12, 29, 30, 31, 48, 49, 50, 52, 54, 55, 89, 90, 98, 99, 102, 111, 128, 154, 166, 173, 174, 180

Apps, 11, 12, 13, 14, 17, 18, 23, 25, 31, 33, 38, 47, 53, 56, 72, 80, 93, 95, 96, 98, 99, 102, 104, 106, 128, 130, 142, 145, 148, 151, 152, 153, 154, 156, 157, 171, 173, 174, 176, 179

B

Bluetooth, 14, 79, 82, 114, 131, 176

C

Calculator, 98
Calculator, 98
Cleanup, 36, 95
Cleanup, 95
Commands, 42, 97, 100, 118
Compressed file, 38, 157
Control Panel, 41, 42, 44, 45, 93, 133
CPU, 6, 55, 56, 107, 112, 113, 133, 176, 177
Customize, 28, 34, 49, 71, 83, 113, 140

D

Default printer, 144
Default Printer, 144

Design, 16, 30, 31, 68, 97, 98, 99, 180

Desktop, 13, 18, 28, 30, 31, 34, 47, 51, 52, 69, 70, 88, 99, 100, 101, 102, 107, 111, 126, 128, 130, 155, 160, 169, 173, 175

Display, 11, 20, 30, 132, 159, 168, 169

Domains, 116

Download, 9, 12, 19, 22, 23, 24, 42, 91, 94, 101, 102, 104, 110, 112, 113, 126, 129, 130, 138, 156, 166, 173, 175

Driver, 11, 19, 94, 131, 157, 171, 172

E

ESRAM, 156

F

Features, 9, 12, 14, 15, 16, 18, 35, 42, 47, 49, 50, 82, 96, 98, 99, 100, 128, 132, 133, 140, 151, 153, 155, 156, 157, 158, 159, 171, 174, 179

File Explorer, 25, 41, 42, 61, 97, 99, 105, 113, 166

Folders, 25, 38, 39

G

Graphics card, 56, 169

H

HDD, 7, 175, 179
Hidden files, 39
History, 34, 68, 73, 74, 103, 107, 142, 149, 175, 176

I

Icons, 27, 28, 34, 35, 37, 39, 45, 49, 51, 71, 80, 91, 92, 97, 100, 124, 163, 169

Install, 12, 19, 20, 21, 33, 34, 42, 53, 92, 97, 102, 104, 109, 110, 112, 113, 128, 129, 130,

138, 139, 140, 145, 154, 155, 156, 157, 158, 166, 167, 169, 173, 174, 175
Internet Security, 153, 154, 159
IP addresses, 107, 118, 119

K

Keyboard, 14, 45, 48, 68, 69, 71, 72, 74, 75, 76, 78, 82, 87, 91, 92, 105, 109, 141, 147, 159, 162, 165, 170, 171, 175

L

Laptops, 89
Layout, 14, 16, 31, 72, 76, 78, 106, 173

M

Menu, 12, 14, 25, 31, 32, 33, 38, 39, 41, 42, 47, 54, 57, 64, 65, 72, 76, 79, 82, 83, 85, 88, 89, 90, 91, 92, 93, 94, 95, 97, 99, 100, 101, 104, 105, 106, 108, 115, 127, 128, 130, 135, 137, 140, 144, 147, 151, 154, 159, 160, 166, 167, 169, 173, 174, 175, 179
Microsoft Edge, 14, 82, 98, 100, 101, 124, 174

N

Network, 52, 57, 103, 107, 116, 118, 119, 120, 122, 126, 127, 146, 148, 149, 154, 159

O

Operating system, 9, 48, 49, 50, 62, 101, 104, 109, 110, 113, 123, 133, 138, 139, 157, 158, 166, 171, 173, 174, 175, 177, 178, 179, 180

P

Password, 44, 109, 110, 116, 120, 122, 127, 146, 147, 148, 150, 151, 152, 157, 175
PASSWORD MANAGER, 6
PC Health Check, 20, 23
Pin, 26, 31, 80, 81, 88, 89, 93, 130, 161, 164
Printers, 116, 144
Privacy setting, 142
Processor, 11, 19, 56, 133, 135, 136, 148, 172

R

RAM, 11, 19, 58, 113, 128, 130, 133, 172
Recent files, 38, 51
Recycle bin, 28, 95
Reinstall, 111, 138, 153

S

Screenshot, 114
Security settings, 140, 147, 148, 153, 154
Setting, 11, 30, 31, 36, 44, 45, 54, 57, 59, 67, 68, 69, 82, 83, 84, 95, 106, 107, 116, 140, 154, 174, 178
Software, 12, 32, 34, 42, 75, 92, 93, 94, 102, 103, 128, 131, 136, 149, 152, 153, 154, 156, 157, 158, 159, 167, 172, 173, 174, 178
Sound settings, 54, 143
SSD, 7, 113, 130, 131, 175, 179
Storage, 11, 19, 26, 57, 58, 59, 67, 113
System Firmware, 19

T

Taskbar, 13, 25, 26, 27, 29, 31, 45, 47, 48, 50, 54, 57, 62, 67, 68, 69, 71, 76, 80, 81, 82, 85, 86, 87, 88, 89, 90, 91, 92, 93, 97, 104, 105, 106, 107, 108, 127, 128, 130, 133, 142, 155, 161, 163, 174
Touch keyboard, 69, 71, 76
Touchscreen, 100
TPM, 11, 19, 107, 113

U

Uninstall, 33, 35, 42, 53, 94
Uninstall, 33, 42, 87, 94
Unpin, 31, 44, 45, 80, 81, 179

V

Voice typing, 75
Volumes, 27, 57, 67
VPN, 6, 126, 127, 128, 159

W

Widgets, 14, 31, 32, 89, 90, 98, 170
Windows, 1, 9, 11, 12, 13, 14, 15, 16, 17, 18, 19, 20, 21, 22, 23, 24, 25, 26, 27, 30, 31, 32, 33, 34, 35, 36, 37, 38, 39, 41, 42, 43, 44, 45, 46, 47, 48, 49, 50, 51, 53, 54, 57, 58, 59, 62,

64, 67, 68, 69, 70, 71, 73, 74, 75, 76, 77, 80,
82, 83, 84, 86, 87, 88, 89, 90, 91, 92, 93, 94,
95, 97, 98, 99, 100, 101, 102, 103, 104, 105,
106, 107, 109, 110, 111, 112, 113, 114, 115,
116, 118, 120, 122, 123, 127, 128, 129, 130,
131, 132, 133, 136, 138, 139, 140, 142, 144,
145, 146, 147, 148, 149, 151, 152, 153, 154,
155, 156, 157, 158, 159, 160, 161, 162, 163,

166, 167, 168, 169, 170, 171, 172, 173, 174,
175, 177, 178, 179, 180

Z

Zip file, 38, 39, 166

Made in the USA
Middletown, DE
13 February 2023

24791123R00104